DAYBOOK

THE JOURNAL OF AN ARTIST

ANNE TRUITT

WITH A NEW INTRODUCTION BY AUDREY NIFFENEGGER

SCRIBNER
NEW YORK LONDON TORONTO SYDNEY NEW DELHI

Scribner
A Division of Simon & Schuster, Inc.
1230 Avenue of the Americas
New York, NY 10020

First Scribner trade paperback edition October 2013

SCRIBNER and design are registered trademarks of The Gale Group, Inc.,
used under license by Simon & Schuster, Inc., the publisher of this work.

For information about special discounts for bulk purchases, please contact Simon
& Schuster Special Sales at 1-866-506-1949 or business@simonandschuster.com.

The Simon & Schuster Speakers Bureau can bring authors to your live event. For
more information or to book an event, contact the Simon & Schuster Speakers
Bureau at 1-866-248-3049 or visit our website at www.simonspeakers.com.

Cover design by Christopher Lin

Cover photograph of the author © annetruitt.org/Bridgeman Art Library

Manufactured in the United States of America

10 9 8 7 6 5 4 3 2 1

Library of Congress Cataloging-in-Publication data is available.

ISBN 978-1-4767-4098-0
ISBN 978-1-4767-4405-6 (ebook)

Lines appear from LETTERS OF RAINER MARIA RILKE: 1892–1910,
translated by Jane Bannard Greene and M. D. Herter Norton. Copyright 1945
by W. W. Norton & Company, Inc., renewed © 1972 by M. D. Herter Norton.
Used by permission of W. W. Norton & Company, Inc.

For Alexandra, Mary, and Sam

Introduction

It's a privilege to be invited into an artist's studio. In *Daybook*, Anne Truitt offers up more: her daily life, her thoughts on the making of art, her childhood, her worries (financial, aesthetic, maternal), as well as her studio practice. Her book is a rare and intense offering, a chance to contemplate the joys and sacrifices artists experience.

When I first read *Daybook* I was an art student. My copy of the book has its yellowed bookmark from the bookshop where I bought it, long defunct. I was a punk girl with magenta hair and a uniform of black trench coat and fishnet stockings; that girl is gone too, replaced by a lady professor who needs reading glasses. But *Daybook* remains; its thoughtful, cogent sentences are unaltered. My need, my understanding of Anne Truitt's experience has changed, though.

As an art student I was searching for women artists who were contrary, steely-minded, committed. I wanted to know how they managed their lives, how they stuck with their art. Art seemed like a difficult calling: How did these women continue, year after year? How did they remain faithful to art?

Now I come to *Daybook* with different questions. What is success, for an artist? How does an artist's personal life influence her art? What is lost and gained as the artist reaches middle age and looks back over her body of work? What does she see when she looks ahead?

Anne Truitt was tough. She considered her life and her art unsparingly. She did her best to present all her selves—artist, teacher, mother, child, divorced woman, breadwinner, and eventually grandmother—integrated or in conflict, as the events of the day demanded. She was born in 1921 and was associated with both the Minimalism and Color Field movements, but was quite independent in her development as an artist. In *Daybook* she describes her decision to become an artist, and her training, which was figurative and grounded in the natural world. She describes a visit to the Guggenheim Museum in New York, where she saw her first Barnett Newman painting: "My whole self lifted into it." She went home and began to make the sculptures that were the beginning of her mature work.

Daybook was written just after Anne Truitt had a retrospective exhibit at the Corcoran Gallery of Art. Retrospectives are strange experiences for any artist. The art is considered, curated, gathered, and shown in a manner that attempts to be definitive. But if the artist is alive, it can be uncomfortable to be defined. So the journal begins in discomfort and becomes an attempt to regroup, to understand. She writes: "The most demanding part of living a lifetime as an artist is the strict discipline of forcing oneself to work steadfastly along the nerve of one's own most intimate sensitivity."

In 2009 I was able to see Anne Truitt's work for the first time. The Hirshhorn Museum in Washington, D.C., her home city, organized a posthumous exhibition of her work; she had died in 2004. I was with my editor Nan Graham, who was a friend and editor to Anne Truitt. Walking between the human-scale columns with their subtle colors, I felt humble and bereft. The maker of these sculptures had shaped my ideas about living; I would have liked to thank her. I looked at Nan and thought about the ways we all change each other, the ineffable transfer of experience, wisdom, and love from person to person.

Anne Truitt made art and wrote books. She kept making art until a month before her death. She had a family and she recorded both her creative and her quotidian life, not only in *Daybook* but in two subsequent books, *Turn* and *Prospect*. Her thoughts are still relevant, not only for artists but for creative people of all disciplines.

Her words and her art continue to resonate.

—*Audrey Niffenegger*
February 4, 2013

Preface

In December 1973, and in April 1974, I was given retrospective exhibits of my work in sculpture and drawing: the first at the Whitney Museum of American Art in New York, the second at the Corcoran Gallery of Art in Washington, D.C., where I live. Walter Hopps was the curator of both exhibits; that is, he reviewed all my work in the most minute detail and, with my cooperation, chose which works were to be shown, and installed the exhibits.

The force of this concentrated and unprecedented attention to my work, and to me, swept over me like a tidal wave. The objects that I had been making for years and years were drawn into visibility and, many of them for the first time, set forth to the public eye. But it was not this aspect of the situation which confounded me. The works stood clear, each in its own space, intact. It was I myself who, the longer and the more intensely we worked, failed to stand clear. I felt crazed, as china is crazed, with tiny fissures. It slowly dawned on me that the more visible my work became, the less visible I grew to myself. In a deeply unsettling realization, I began to see that I had used the process of art not only to contain my intensities but also to exorcize those beyond my endurance, and must have done so with haste akin to panic, for it was a kind of panic I felt when once again inexorably confronted by my own work. Confronted, actually, by the reactivation of feelings I had thought to get rid of forever, now so objectified that I felt myself brutalized by them, defenseless because I had depended on objectification for defense. I also felt that my failure to come to terms with these feelings as I was making the work had deprived me of myself in these most profound depths. It was as if the artist in me had ravished the rest of me and got away scot-free. I had the curious feeling of being brought personally to justice, but obliquely.

These feelings made no sense to me until I came slowly and painfully to the conviction that, although I had been scrupulous in trying to integrate the other areas of my life, I had avoided confrontation with the artist.

This anguish overwhelmed me until, early one morning and quite without emphasis, it occurred to me that I could simply record my life for one year and see what happened. So I bought a brown notebook like the ones in which I made lecture notes in college, chose a special day (the first of a visit to a friend in Arizona), and began to write, sitting up in bed every morning and writing for as long a time as seemed right. The only limitation I set was to let the artist speak. My hope was that if I did this honestly I would discover how to see myself from a perspective that would render myself whole in my own eyes.

As I wrote, my life continued in its ordinary round. I took care of my three children, Alexandra, Mary, and Sam, who at the time (1974) were nineteen, sixteen, and fourteen. I cooked and cleaned and gardened and did all the various duties that fall to the lot of a woman living with her children alone. I tried to be patient with the rhythmical unfolding of my writing, never to second-think it, and as the year went on found myself rewarded when a subtle logic began to emerge. I began to see how my life had made itself as I was living it, how naturally and inevitably I had become an artist.

In 1978 my first grandchild was born and I felt moved once more to write, this time with the idea that I might be able to illuminate for myself the painful confusion I felt during the transition my children made as they moved into adulthood, away from me.

So this book has come to exist in a natural way. I hope it may just as naturally keep other people company as they live their lives.

—*Yaddo*
September 1981

TUCSON,
ARIZONA
JUNE
1974

6 JUNE

I have come here to Arizona to visit a friend and to rest because I am in need of comfort after the tensions of last winter, which have left me with a tangle: crossed lines of thought and feeling. I had spent months preparing for two retrospective exhibits, one in New York and one in Washington, and the course of events was much too swift for understanding. I just had to keep winding it all up, every which way. In Kyōto I once saw women rinsing dyed cloths in the Kamo River. The unwieldy lengths of cloth rippled out in long ribbons of blue and green and yellow and orange and red. The river rushed over the colors, the cloth whipped in the swift waves, the women held on to the streamers for dear life. It was a desperate business. I feel as desperate about the unwinding of all that happened to me so fast.

Flying over the desert yesterday, I found myself lifted out of my preoccupations by noticing suddenly that everything was curved. Seen whole from the air, circumscribed by its global horizon, the earth confronted me bluntly as a context all its own, echoing that grand sweep. I had the startling impression that I was looking at something intelligent. Every delicate pulsation of color was met, matched, challenged, repulsed, embraced by another, none out of proportion, each at once unique and a proper part of the whole. The straight lines with which human beings have marked the land are impositions of a different intelligence, abstract in this arena of the natural. Looking down at these facts, I began to see my life as somewhere between these two orders of the natural and the abstract, belonging entirely neither to the one nor to the other.

In my work as an artist I am accustomed to sustaining such tensions: a familiar position between my senses, which are natural, and my intuition of an order they both mask and illuminate. When I draw a straight line or conceive of an arrangement of tangible elements all my own, I inevitably impose my own order on matter. I actualize this order, rendering it accessible to my senses. It is not so accessible until actualized.

An eye for this order is crucial for an artist. I notice that as I live from day to day, observing and feeling what goes on both inside and outside myself, certain aspects of what is happening adhere to me, as if magnetized by a center of psychic gravity. I have learned to trust this center, to rely on its acuity and to go along with its choices although the center itself remains mysterious to me. I sometimes feel as if I *recognize* my own experience. It is a feeling akin to that of unexpectedly meeting a friend in a strange place, of being at once startled and satisfied—startled to find outside myself what feels native to me, satisfied to be so met. It is exhilarating.

I have found that this process of selection, over which I

have virtually no control, isolates those aspects of my experience that are most essential to me in my work because they echo my own attunement to what life presents me. It is as if there are external equivalents for truths which I already in some mysterious way know. In order to catch these equivalents, I have to stay "turned on" all the time, to keep my receptivity to what is around me totally open. Preconception is fatal to this process. Vulnerability is implicit in it; pain, inevitable.

7 JUNE

Sometimes I yearn to "turn off." I wish I could live in a lower key in a place like the mobile home court through which I walked last evening during a windy, desert-smelling twilight. A makeshift human habitation loosely connected by winding, homemade paths. "Hello" called here and there by a man leaning over his car, by another accompanying his wife, who carried a plate of cookies. A woman watering her lawn (about two feet square) remarked that it was windy. I said it looked like rain. She said she hoped it would. I said, yes, we've had a drought. Nothing much, all this, but everything too: usual and, because so, comforting.

8 JUNE

My hand is out. I feel it a numb weight hanging off my right arm as if no longer quick with life. The marks on my fine-grained drawing paper are simply marks, physical traces as meaningless as chicken tracks in the dirt. This is not a new thing to me and is, I suppose, the analogue of writer's block. Some vital connection in my spirit has gone flaccid. I have learned over the years (there is always the frightening shadow—is it forever?) how to behave. Rest is a concept that seems easy to understand, but I do not find it so, for it is precisely those overstrained parts of myself that persist most obstinately to jangle.

Yet, for all the strains of the retrospectives, I am most profoundly grateful to have had the opportunity to *see* my work. There were radiant moments. Like the night at the Corcoran Gallery of Art when Walter Hopps and I walked into the room in which we were preparing the exhibit. The sculptures stood in long rows, barely visible, lit only dimly by a skylight. We did not turn on the lights. I walked up and down the dark corridors between their massive forms, most of which towered over me, and held out both my hands to feel them, not touching them. They stood in their own space, in their own time, and I was glad in their presence.

9 JUNE

Consciousness seems to me increasingly inconceivable. I know more and more that I know nothing of its nature, range, and force except what I experience through the slot of this physical body. The tie to my body may *feel* stronger than it *is*. So it seems anyway when I remember how I occasionally hold myself separate from it. Yet I balk. When we love one another the most delicate truth of that love is held in the spirit, but my body is the record of those I have loved. I feel their bones as my bones, almost literally. This record is autonomous. It continues, dumbly, to persist. Its power is independent of time. The love is fixed, instantly accessible to memory, somehow stained into my body as color into cloth.

All bodies have this record. It is the magic of drawing them. Here, where my pencil touches the paper, is the place at which a body holds itself intact. The line marks, with infinite tenderness, the experience of a body—a separate unknowable experience inside the line, space outside it.

It was the record of this experience that I was after in the late forties and the early fifties when I modeled human bodies. Classical beauty held no interest for me. I pursued the marks of experience, the lines and lumps left by physical and psychological events assimilated with such difficulty that they had made permanent plastic changes. *Elvira,* made in 1952 and now destroyed, held her head high over her drained chest; her eyes protruded in a clumsy effort to see what had happened to her. Her hair clung to her head, bunched into an earnest knot at the nape of her stretched neck. She moved out of herself under my hands and then stopped, struck into a stasis she could just barely maintain, a balance so precariously wrought that it had consumed all her vital force.

When I was told, before my marriage, that I was sterile and would never be able to bear children, the deprivation of this palpably physical knowledge haunted and wrenched me; I knew that what I wanted to know for myself had to be known physically. I could not, and did not, accept the fate of remaining as I was then, a woman unmarked by experience, inviolate at my deepest roots. When I modeled one marked, used female body after another, I was recording adumbrations of what I have now, at the age of fifty-three, become. The sculpture failed as art because I did not know at the time, and could not guess except dimly, how much vital force is garnered in the course of assimilating experience. The meaning the sculpture conveyed was skewed toward pain; wrenched proportions twisted it toward caricature. The just proportion of classical form is, I have learned, true to experienced proportion. I now feel my own used body as whole, replete with lines and lumps, but also with a vitality they serve to mark.

I 3   J U N E

A woman is lost in the desert. A young policeman came to ask us to watch out for her. Senile—"she won't know where she is"—110 pounds, 5'1", in a sleeveless one-piece yellow dress with red and green flowers on it. She belongs in a nursing home about half a mile away across the desert. We all know she will not be able to survive the heat, about 100°. "She won't be in good shape," the policeman said gently. We watch for her but do not see any yellow and red and green spots in the desert.

I 4   J U N E

Last night, for the first time in many weeks, I truly slept. I woke once to listen to the little noises of the desert night, and later, chilly in dawn, to pull over me a thin white woolen blue-monogrammed blanket. I had forgotten what sleep is like—a kingdom all its own.

I 5   J U N E

This morning the light struck the back of my hand at such a slant as to evoke plains stretching far away. A Sahara, sand color; camels could have traversed it only in days of travel.

This quick flash took me back to the Saihōji Garden in Kyōto, Japan. There, walking along the paths, which meandered in and out among patches of many varying mosses, my children and I used to play games with scale, wandering in the multifoliate greens clinging to the soft mounds of earth as if in great primeval forests that tangled and roared over our heads.

It has been partly such play with scale that has drawn my attention to the intervals between events, to what is happening when "nothing" is happening. The meaning of two hands clapped is fixed in the soundless interval between the claps. Just so, the meaning of our experience is held in the infinitely short intervals between our sensory perceptions.

It is clearly to be observed in babies and young children. The mother *listens* to her baby. She tunes her neural receivers to the baby's and then is able psychologically to hold her child, to prevent the child's feeling distress. This is the bliss of motherhood, this heavenly capacity to make another human being happy. This same attunement enables the mother to catch her baby's frustrations before they become too painful for the baby to accept. The art of motherhood is to maintain this nimble adjustment to the child's course of experience, catching the intervals in such a way that the child can learn to explore independently without coming to harm.

It is no wonder that a man can feel angry when his children are born and this ineffable communication with the mother is established so visibly. Men must occasionally feel a maddening kind of jealousy, most particularly so because there can be no decent relief. And it must be exacerbated by the intuitive knowledge that this is precisely the kind of tuning that occurs in making love. I did not realize when my babies were born how much his natural exclusion from this state of bliss with them may have hurt my husband. I wish I had. The delight was so whole that it seemed to me that he must be burnished by the same glow, especially as it came from a sun lit by him.

17 JUNE

The old woman is dead. She was found on the desert not far from here.

The young policeman said, "She won't know where she is," but I think she may have known very well. She left the nursing home in the evening—homecoming time on the desert, when all the animals hunker down. The old woman lay down with them.

My hand is still out.

19 JUNE

Concerned as I have been these past months to act as intelligently as I could in a complex situation, I have become alert to the frequency with which people tend to act only in the context of their own assumptions. Certain occurrences can then appear to be proof of these assumptions. A wife may assume, for example, that her husband loves her. This may become the foundation for her own actions and for her interpretation of his actions. If he teases her all the time, it is because he dotes on her idiosyncracies. If he drops his clothes for her to pick up, it is because he delights in her care of him. She forgets that it is only within the context of her assumptions that these actions are affectionate. It is just a step from here to the convenience of abstractions that drain the truth out of our experience, dangerously elevating us above the vital checks and balances of the hurly-burly of life.

I leave Arizona tomorrow and, after a brief interval to check on my household in Washington, will go for two months to Yaddo in Saratoga Springs, New York. There, in the unaccustomed company of other artists, I will work, secluded.

YADDO,
SARATOGA
SPRINGS,
NEW YORK
JULY–AUGUST
1974

I JULY

This household at Yaddo, of which I am now a part, is organized the way my mother organized the household of my childhood. I feel the orderly rolling of routine around me: repetitive, familiar, restorative. Dinner last night was nostalgic, in the perfect balance of nursery food: candied sweet potatoes, a touch of pineapple, peas, cranberry sauce, cottage cheese, a delightful salad, ice cream, and a large glass of milk. The simple joy of childhood rose in me, a joy elicited by food and by welcome into a household of objective routine.

I have the comfortable feeling of being an inconsequential member of a litter, like a puppy or a kitten. I have a place but am not outstanding in any way. This is a feeling I have always enjoyed enormously. It heals me in some subtle way.

My childhood household was too formal to convey the lighthearted feeling of being in a litter. It was not until 1934, when my younger twin sisters and I visited my mother's sister, Aunt Nancy, on her farm outside of Charlottesville, Virginia, that I first encountered the relaxation of being one of many children. At that time, as now, I was overstrained by too much responsibility, too much earnestness, and too much sadness. It is a joy to be here, set free, anonymous within a shelter.

2 JULY

My studio here is peacefully widening out. The green shades are furled, the windows are open onto a sweet-smelling meadow with purple martin houses stalking among fruit trees. A grapevine flourishes against the gray stones of the south wall—the studio is called Stone South—and meanders in tendrils over my screens. A wide vegetable garden lies beyond a stout privet hedge to the east. Two triangular skylights allow the northern light to flood in, and me to see the changing clouds. My drawing table stands free to itself. In another area there is room for two sawhorses to support an 8' X 4' piece of 3/4" plywood on which I can paint, and other surfaces on which I can spread finished work.

My bedroom is small and white and has a turret and a narrow green-tiled adjoining bathroom. I do not have a telephone by my bed, alert for emergency, and I can leave my glasses on my bureau, yards away, when I sleep. Pine-scented wind sings gently within my shell. I am alone, acknowledged in a silent community.

A community as yet mysterious to me. Guests come and go as quixotically as the White Rabbit. Yet we are all drawn together into a kind of tacit intimacy by being artists, which we handle in different ways. We are gently curious about one another, as if we all had the same disease, could compare symptoms and treatments.

My hand is back in. The tourniquet that strain had been twisting around it for the past few months has loosened, and its connection with the part of me that knows how to make work in art is once again vital.

I do not understand why I seem able to make what people call art. For many long years I struggled to learn how to do it, and I don't even know why I struggled. Then, in 1961, at the age of forty, it became clear to me that I was doing work I respected within my own strictest standards. Furthermore, I found this work respected by those whose understanding of art I valued. My first, instinctive reaction to this new situation was, if I'm an artist, being an artist isn't so fancy because it's just me. But now, thirteen years later, there seems to be more to it than that. It isn't "just me." A simplistic attitude toward the course of my life no longer serves.

The "just me" reaction was, I think, an instinctive disavowal of the social role of the artist. A life-saving disavowal. I refused, and still refuse, the inflated definition of artists as special people with special prerogatives and special excuses. If artists embrace this view of themselves, they necessarily have to attend to its perpetuation. They have to live it out. Their time and energy are consumed for social purposes. Artists then make decisions in terms of a role defined by others, falling into their power and serving to illustrate their theories. The Renaissance focused this social attention on the artist's individuality, and the focus persists today in a curious form that on the one hand inflates artists' egoistic concept of themselves and on the other places them at the mercy of the social forces on which they become dependent. Artists can suffer terribly in this dilemma. It is taxing to think out and then maintain a view of one's self that is realistic. The pressure to earn a living confronts a fickle public taste. Artists have to please whim to live on their art. They stand in fearful danger of looking to this taste to define their working decisions. Sometime during the course of their development, they have to forge a character subtle enough to nourish and protect and foster the growth of the part of themselves that makes art, and at the same time practical enough to deal with the world pragmatically. They have to maintain a position between care of themselves and care of their work in the world, just as they have to sustain the delicate tension between intuition and sensory information.

This leads to the uncomfortable conclusion that artists *are*, in this sense, special because they are intrinsically involved in a difficult balance not so blatantly precarious in other professions. The lawyer and the doctor *practice* their callings. The plumber and the carpenter *know* what they will be called upon to do. They do not have to spin their work out of themselves, discover its laws, and then present themselves turned inside out to the public gaze.

4 JULY

Yesterday's effort—a long day of demanding work in the studio—seems to have triggered a familiar state. I woke up in the middle of last night hot, flustered, nauseated, and dried out. I had counted prematurely on reserve energy. And now, as in Parcheesi, I am back at Home Start again. I am thankful to be here at Yaddo, where I can stay in bed without disturbing anyone, or anyone's even knowing.

What worries me is that I try so hard to be sensitive to the variations in my energy level, and fail so often. It frightens me that my children's security is dependent on my unsturdy, unstable body. Also, the preemptive images that present themselves to me in my conception of my work are on a scale way out of proportion to my capacity to bring them into being. My hand is securely in. My working program was brought into order yesterday. All my projects are on schedule, with the delightful prospect of open time at the end for painting on canvas. But today I am jerked back by the reins of my own physical weakness.

Perhaps the human lesson is always submission. We have a choice: to rebel or to recognize our powerlessness while maintaining our faith. In my own case, the first choice is denied me. I simply haven't the energy. What rebellion is possible for me emerges as febrile depression. My preconception of how events should go has tricked me once more; I must try to open myself to the flow of cause and effect (of which I am such a small part) with a clean, trusting simplicity.

So I will try to behave intelligently. A day of solitude in bed with *The Golden Bowl* will probably restore me to work. And I hope I will be here long enough to soak up reserve strength.

5 JULY

The separation of mind and body seems to appear most distinctly after an illness ends. My mind, now clear, is back in the studio, leans over my drawing board, and turns to consider the progress of the sculptures. If it were on its own, I would intently walk over there and intently work. My body walks to the desk and back to bed, glad to return.

Balancing intuition against sensory information, and sensitivity to one's self against pragmatic knowledge of the world, is not a stance unique to artists. The specialness of artists is the degree to which these precarious balances are crucial backups for their real endeavor. Their essential effort is to catapult themselves wholly, without holding back one bit, into a course of action without having any idea where they will end up. They are like riders who gallop into the night, eagerly leaning on their horse's neck, peering into a blinding rain. And they have to do it over and over again. When they find that they have ridden and ridden—maybe for years, full tilt—in what is for them a mistaken direction, they must unearth within themselves some readiness to turn direction and to gallop off again. They may spend a little time scraping off the mud, resting the horse, having a hot bath, laughing and sitting in candlelight with friends. But in the back of their minds they never forget that the dark, driving run is theirs to make again. They need their balances in order to support their risks. The more they develop an understanding of all their experience—the more it is at their command—the more they carry with them into the whistling wind.

There seems to be a law that the more conscious knowledge you develop, the more you can expand your consciousness. The artist takes advantage of this law. Wise artists like Titian and Rembrandt and Matisse became greater as they became older. Piero della Francesca died blind at the age of ninety-odd. I think often of what he must have kept on seeing, his own space and color perfectly balanced and alive behind his fixed eyes.

The central fact of the dark run is its high emotion, and this is in no way avoidable in actually making a work of art, even when—as happened to me early this morning—the *look* of what you are trying to make is clear in your mind's eye. A certain train of thought that absorbed me ten years ago resurfaced about 5 a.m. in the form of a series of drawings and paintings so plain in their essence that I wonder they evaded me for so long.

This work, which I will begin to make today, is a shear turn of my own earth. When Walter Hopps and I worked on my retrospective last winter, his dogged insistence that I search out every extant piece of work I ever put my hand on plowed, cross-plowed, and replowed this field. The process was unbelievably painful, but I had to watch it happen. Are you sure there weren't some drawings in 1958 after Mary was born? What happened to the Tokyo work of spring 1967? Where is it? Is it in the basement? Is it on that shelf in the basement? What's up there, that package? What's in that box? What's behind that box? He even forced me to remember three little sculptures I had totally forgotten doing in 1963, because he *felt* I had made them: three I had forgotten for reasons so close to my psychological bone that I had to stop talking for a moment to collect myself before saying, yes, I had made them, they are here and there, of these dimensions and colors and so forth. He was merciless. He never relented for a second in his intent to see *everything*.

He exposed year after year of labor. We saw together the character of my effort, as lucid as the annular rings of a tree's growth. He was like the Hound of Heaven. I felt it that way.

I fled. He followed—and followed and followed. His intuitive leap to the certainty of a gap in the work's natural development prodded my reluctant memory over and over again. Until finally there came an end. "Now you can stockpile again," he said, and departed from my studio, leaving me as tenderly clean as a wind-washed shell.

The core of my reluctance was, of course, cowardice. I had recorded in order to forget. I had hustled my pain, my despair, my delight, my bafflement onto paper and into clay and wood and stone, and fixed them there as if in magic enchantment. I had thought to hold them, beyond reexamination, reexperience. Sprung from my deliberately wrought tombs, my most secret feelings arose alive, bleeding and dazzling, to overwhelm me once more. I simply could not believe what was happening. And all the while I was in the full midstream of events, decisions to be made, children to be cared for, meals to be cooked, the house to be cleaned, friends to be cherished.

Paradoxically, it was this very pressure that saved me. My past meshed into my present. It had to be taken in, considered, woven. I found, to my surprise, that the experience of my twenties, thirties, and forties had room in my fifties. The warp and woof of my self was looser and stronger than I had known. Thinking I would not survive, I found myself enriched by myself.

9 JULY

My work is coming steadily along. My pace in the studio is practiced. I move from one task to another with the ease of Tarzan swinging on lianas through the jungle. I am at once totally in jeopardy and totally at home.

On the edge of awakening this morning, I slid into the happy consciousness that my life here is just right. I thrive in the repetitive routine. Innocent pleasures suit me. I continue to feel as safe as a younger child in a large family.

My mother's cool handling of childhood crises was one of my first lessons in how to live. Once I was bitten by a black snake. Blackberry bushes grew close to the dirt road at Lee Haven, a house near Easton, Maryland, in which we spent a summer when I was about seven. Moving through deceptively soft-looking wild grasses that prickled my legs, and picking and eating as I went, I was pushing farther and farther into the thicket when suddenly I felt a blunt, muscular hit on my leg, a sharp pain, and in that second saw the snake's black body whip out of sight. I remember a moment of paralysis as my seven-year-old mind organized the facts. Then I ran, crying and calling for my mother, to the dark-shingled, frightening house (overshadowed by tall pines, never sunlit), up the white steps onto the wooden porch, in through the wide front door and into the central hall. My mother, in her light cotton dress and white sneakers, was by that time running down the staircase to meet me.

With no loss of time whatsoever and with equally no hurry, she looked at the mark, asked a couple of clear questions about the snake's body, made me lie down on the black, horsehair sofa in the dining room, told the nurse to put some wet soda cloths on my leg, and called the doctor. I can see her now, dignified and reserved as always, with the telephone receiver shaped like a black tulip held to her ear.

My father was always more anxious about me than my

mother. He returned home later that afternoon and rounded the corner into the dining room at a fast trot, flushed with concern and love. Comfortable by that time, I was complacently changing my own wet soda cloths.

I cannot remember ever not knowing that my father loved me more than anyone in the world. I abided in that love, loved and honored it as he loved and honored me. But I never truly understood this central stove of warmth and light in my life until long after my father was dead, until I reached the age he had been in my childhood. Because I was born when he was forty-two, it is only in the last few years that I have wholly loved him. When I was younger, his love seemed excessive, embarrassing because of a proportion I could meet only decorously, never realistically.

It was my mother's cooler hand that guided, apparently effortlessly and rather unemotionally, my efforts to learn how to live.

14 JULY

Three sculptures are finished, small ones: *Parva* I, II, and III. And I have now started a series of drawings I am calling *Stone South*. These are pencil and white paint, very spare: attempts to catch the threshold of consciousness, the point at which the abstract nature of events becomes perceptible. This comes down to the placement of interval: lines meeting and not meeting as close as the force of their lengths will allow; a metaphor for the virtually imperceptible ways in which our lives turn, critical turns of change determined by interval.

I have settled into the most comfortable routine I have ever known in my working life. I wake very early and, after a quiet period, have my breakfast in my room: cereal, fruit, nuts, the remainder of my luncheon thermos of milk, and coffee. Then I write in my notebook in bed. By this time, the sun is well up and the pine trees waft delicious smells into my room. My whole body sings with the knowledge that nothing is expected of me except what I expect of myself. I dress, do my few room chores, walk to the mansion to pick up my lunch box (a sandwich, double fruit, double salad—often a whole head of new lettuce) and thermos of milk, and walk down the winding road to my Stone South studio.

At noon, I stop working, walk up through the meadow to West House, have a reading lunch at my desk, and nap. By 2:30 or so I am back in the studio. Late in the afternoon, I return to my room, have a hot bath and dress for dinner. It is heavenly to work until I am tired, knowing that the evening will be effortless. Dinner is a peaceful pleasure. Afterward I usually return to my solitude, happy to have been in good company, happy to leave it. I read, or write letters, have another hot bath in the semidarkness of my room, and sink quietly to sleep.

I 5 JULY

My mother's moral force radiated from her like a gentle pulsation. Sensitive people picked it up and found her presence delicately satisfying. Tall, slender, light-boned, fair-skinned, everything about her was fined down almost to transparency. She moved over the ground lightly, and her golden brown hair (never cut until her head was shaved for an operation to excise the brain tumor that was already killing her) was piled up softly and allowed to fall over her high forehead, above which it seemed to float. Fine, like the rest of her, it would have radiated like an aureole around her head had she not decisively worn a net, invisible, made of real hair.

She was herself only when alone. I used to watch her brace herself for people; even, occasionally, for me. And then watch her straight, narrow back relax, her shoulders drop a little, as she set out for a walk. A few steps away from the house and her feet would begin to skim.

This satisfaction with being solitary was a tremendous source of freedom for me. It implied a delight in self and affirmed my own obsessive sieving of experience. By taking her mind totally off me, she gave me my own autonomy. I knew from experience that she was careful and responsible. I realized that she would have watched me had she not been sure that I was all right. And, if she were sure, I could be sure. Very early in my life, I set out stoutly to look around at everything.

The brick kilns down the street from my house were my first experience of how things were made. They stood on an open lot: low domes with rectangular doors through which, at my level, I looked directly into intense fire—a color unlike anything I had seen before in nature. The bricks went into the kilns fresh and cool and came out dried, hot, and hard. It took me time to grasp this process. I had to return over and over again to see it and to piece the sequence together. Too young to ask, I simply kept going back until I understood.

And so it was with the little town of Easton, on Maryland's Eastern Shore: an orderly scattering of houses, mostly white clapboard, so small that even on my short legs I was able to encompass the town's dimensions.

The exercise of this childhood faculty to make a map by simply experiencing the space of an area made Tokyo, where I lived from 1964 to 1967, fascinating to me. There were few street signs, and these I ignored in order to enjoy learning how it all pieced together; in the beginning, I rode in taxis looking out the back window so I could identify my return route. Once routes were established, they formed sections, and these sections finally connected. I devised a web for myself of intertwining, crooked, and elusive roads in which I could live. Yet I never came to feel at home in Japan, hard as I tried. I simply felt incorrectly placed. The air seemed to lack oxygen; the latitude and longitude were incompatible; I felt myself to be in the wrong place on the earth.

Coming into Yaddo has made me realize how dependent I am on this kind of psychological and physical knowledge of where I am. My adjustment here has been a speeded-up run of an old pattern. As a child, I used to lie at night in the Yellow Room at Avonlea, under the roof of loving and loved friends, and feel a flood of homesick desolation, followed by the physical settling of my body into the lumpy mattress. This comforted me. In my body I knew where I was. I would gaze blindly around the darkened room, placing the furniture where I knew it to be from the daytime. The head of the bed backed into a window overlooking a broad lawn that dropped abruptly off into the Tred Avon River. Pallid gray light would begin to fill the room as my eyes adapted to the night. I would turn on my mattress, fitting more securely into it. Spreading beyond the windows behind my head, stretched the lawn, the river, and, following that to the east and north, the town where my house was, my parents, my sisters. I would drift off to sleep, in place.

This dependence on placement is ingrained in me. I pay attention to latitude and longitude. It's as if the outside world has to match some personal horizontal and vertical axis. I have to line up with it in order to be comfortable.

When I was looking for a house in Tokyo, I was confronted by textural uniformity. There were no residential areas. Everything was interlocked in a repetitive pattern. I felt like a weary seabird trying to decide which wave to alight on in a choppy ocean.

I strained for a state in which I could feel myself placed, and my children safely placed with me.

2 1 J U L Y

Sculptors, relying as they do on subtle kinaesthetic cues for the apprehension of weight and form, may be more dependent than other people on placement. I place myself in Washington, almost precisely on the cross of latitude and longitude of Baltimore, where I was born, and of the Eastern Shore of Maryland where I grew up. David Smith, the only other sculptor whom I have known well, chose Bolton Landing, which I visited a few days ago.

For all his apparent toughness, his closely fibered flesh and heavy bones and bristly hair, David was, I always felt, totally vulnerable. He would resist—he tended to keep a field of *noli me tangere* around himself—and he would fight, but he felt it all. Like a bull walrus, he was crisscrossed with old hurts.

David's presence was physically comforting, his bulk loomed so. And his intelligence was formidable. He focused it on his art and, like sun through a glass, it could ignite. He seemed never to forget that he was an artist. He just plain chose not to. His professional generosity was total. He taught me the importance of immediately signing and dating every piece of work. He put my attention on how I signed my name. One day in my studio, he grabbed an old scrub brush, marked it with a stroke of white paint, and scratched his name and date into the paint, offering me his way of signing. When I had fabrication difficulties, he suggested technical changes. He accepted me into the honorable family of artists, which he once said was "the only true aristocracy," and he challenged me to be the "best goddamned artist in the world." In the next breath he might wonder out loud whether his toe-protector shoes were really strong enough. Or speak with fear—not, it seemed, for himself, but for his work—of not living long. When asked by other artists to critique their work, David always said it was fine, encouraging them no matter what he thought about the quality of their work, because he felt he had no business discouraging anyone who might be able to be an artist.

In January of 1965, I flew from Tokyo to New York for my second exhibit at the André Emmerich Gallery. I landed at night, fourteen hours straight out of the east, and went immediately to Kenneth Noland's retrospective opening at the Jewish Museum. I felt dazed. All the familiar people were still going on. It was like the last chapter of *À la Recherche du Temps Perdu,* except that it seemed to be I who had died. David asked me how I liked Japan. I said I didn't. He looked disappointed in me, began to speak about Japanese art, looked at me again, then leant down and very gently kissed my cheek.

That was the last time I saw David, and after his death the studio felt lonelier. I came to understand that David's essence for me was that while he was alive he was working. And, if he were working, I was not alone.

One of my mother's bequests to me was the idea of making things run smoothly. It was engrained in me very, very early that I was not only to make as little fuss as possible myself but also to soothe anyone else who was fussing, and further-more to watch intently for the first sign of situations giving rise to fussing in order to forestall them. This concern was partly temperamental—my mother was delicately calibrated emotionally—and partly traditional. This curve of control matched, convex to concave, her independence of spirit. Her life was lived on its spine, and mine followed. We paid for our independence inside by doing things well outside.

One step further lurked the pit of hypocrisy: thinking one way and acting another. We avoided this, more or less suc-cessfully, in two ways. The first was by taking care all the time to rationalize events into what could be handled smoothly. I can remember watching my mother doing this, both in the drawing room and in the nursery. She chose which aspects of a disagreeable situation she would address herself to, and isolated them as artfully as if life were a game of jackstraws. By this kind of manipulation, we tried to define the course of our lives in accordance with our ideas of what we could handle. We kept our actions honest by the complicated effort of constantly defining what we thought about them.

The second guardrail against the pit was a principle much stronger than that of not making a fuss. In the interest of this principle—that intellectual honesty was the bedrock of a life bestowed by God—making a fuss was sometimes crucial. This life, a gift of grace for an unknown reason, must be lived purely, because at death we return with its accruements to our source. Life is entrusted to us, does not belong to us, and has to be restored in honorable condition. We are responsible for this trust, and must live with this fact in mind.

Wherever we stood, my mother and I, we placed ourselves as upright as possible with God above us and the earth under our feet, trying to forget neither.

It has taken me many years to recognize the mistake intrinsic to my mother's approach to shouldering this responsibility: She never developed a faith in natural process strong enough to allow herself to trust it, and herself to it. She permitted the circumstances of her life to wear her out while she gracefully maintained a self-defined position in a self-limited world.

I was, I think, more fortunate. In the fullness of my middle years, at the age of forty-three, just when I stood most in danger of stiffening into my mother's pattern, my husband's career led us to Japan, where I was unable to play the jackstraws game. None of the straws, neither personal nor environmental, could be sufficiently detached for me to control them.

I felt this defeat adumbrated from the air as our plane banked sharply to land in March 1964, and I saw beneath me a wrinkled-prune land, purple in an apricot-violet mist of evening light. A shock of astonishment flashed through every cell of my body: an instinctive realization that nothing in my experience would help me now, but everything in my experience must be in readiness to learn. In that second, something in me went numb. It was as if the jackstraws game had enabled me to meet the demands of ordinary life and to maintain a kind of structural fence within which I could endure the emotional intensity of my work. Without this security, I became frightened. Though I continued to live from day to day as intelligently as I could, the vital force from which my work had been steadily emerging since 1961 simply stopped. Deprived of this natural flow, as well as of my emotional courage, I was driven to make my work with my mind and its quality so dropped that when I was preparing for the retrospectives last winter I destroyed all the sculpture I had made in Japan. It was simply intelligent work, lifeless.

Looking back, I am astonished that I continued to work at all. Something stubborn and dumb in myself had taken over. I worked harder than I had ever worked in my life, had to work harder because so often the sculpture, varied in a neo-constructivist manner out of a desperate intellectual preoccupation with the laws of visual experience, had to be stripped of color several times before I could even get near to what I thought—thought, not felt—I wanted. A complicating element was the light in Japan, entirely different from that of the United States. When I brought sculptures from Japan to New York for exhibition in 1965, I was horrified to see that the color looked wrong. And I was so out of touch with myself that I used aluminum instead of my customary wood for my structures.

The emotional telepathy of the Japanese penetrated my spirit. I had all my life been accustomed to feeling alien. In Japan, I *was* alien. And made to feel it. Most particularly by an old woman who lived a few doors up the alley from my studio. My studios have always meant home to me in a special way, so I was painfully vulnerable to her unrelenting hostility, which felt to me like murder. In all the four years we spent as neighbors, she never once returned my greeting, nor even raised her eyes to mine—except on a single occasion and then only to give me a piercing wound. Her entire waking life was spent, apparently, on her front doorstep. All day long she sat there surrounded by piles and piles of old magazines and papers over which she pored endlessly. Around her spread a pool of dark feeling as palpable as smoke. It was difficult for me to take in the facts of her existence. In snow and rain, in heat, from early to late, she never moved except for the shift of an arm, and that I saw only once or twice as a scarcely identifiable movement of her heavy black garments. There was simply nothing to be done about her existence; I could neither help her in her obviously dire poverty nor alter the fact that her attitude toward me wiped out my own existence.

So, unlike my mother, whose ramparts were never breached, I suffered a frightening rout of my habitual defenses. My fortress was indeed so inundated that I was forced to abandon it. I lost forever a whole methodology of living, including my faith in forming such a methodology. Very slowly and painfully, the thrust of my effort to live my life responsibly moved from the habitual formation of constructions to a simple observation that opened my eyes to the natural flow of events. I was forced to grant grace to natural process, myself naked in it, and my life began to present itself in its own rhythm. At first tentatively and then with more confidence, I began to find delight in acquiescence, and finally even a kind of joy in acceptance.

From 1948, when I decided to enter the Institute of Contemporary Art in Washington as a student in sculpture, to 1961, when my work suddenly took an autonomous turn, the forces of instinct and the forces of intuition fought for control of my work. Yesterday intuition fell back briefly before instinct. My hand wanted to *draw*, to run free. Colors overran, lines tilted, and with about the same degree of effectiveness as Don Quixote going at the windmills. For one whole day I entertained the notion, which had been creeping up on me, of turning my back on the live nerve of myself and *having fun*.

This morning I am sober. I would be a fool to sacrifice joy to fun.

I now have two large plywood surfaces in Stone South and am working on them in tandem so that the series of paintings on canvas I am calling *Brunt* is coming along rapidly. They are coming out of the shear turn that presented itself to my inner eye a few weeks ago, a return to the preoccupations in my early sixties' sculpture: burnt umbers; blacks; dark, dark reds and blues and purples rammed into proportions allowing, to my eye, no room for potential change. They are for me as categorically restrictive as endurance; they are the brunt of endurance. A familiar brunt. It was only in 1967, in the exhilaration of my return from Japan to America, that it occurred to me that I could use the energy I had been putting into endurance to *change* my life. Yet the concept of brunt, of accepting and enduring, still seems to me to have a kind of nobility. It is, perhaps, less intelligent, but there is a stubborn selfhood about it that is dear to me. It can be, quite literally, the only way to survive.

I am only just now realizing how inorganic, unnatural, my work is. Like the straight lines on the desert, what is clearest in me bears no relation to what I see around me. This is paradoxical, since everything I make in the studio is a distillation of direct experience, sometimes even specific visual experience. *Nanticoke,* which I've never been able to make, is two whole instantaneous "takes" of a bridge and marsh on the Eastern Shore of Maryland, one from childhood superimposed by a second from adulthood. Someday, I hope, these will fuse and come through definitively.

The terms of the experience and the terms of the work itself are totally different. But if the work is successful—I cannot ever know whether it is or not—the experience becomes the work and, through the work, is accessible to others with its original force.

For me, this process is mysterious. It's like not knowing where you're going but knowing how to get there. The fifteen years that David Smith thought it took to become an artist are spent partly in learning how to move ahead sure-footedly as if you did actually know where you are going.

Along one of the roads here at Yaddo, a tall pine and a beech tree have grown so close to one another that the beech's limbs have been diverted by the pine's trunk. They jut out from joints swollen to uphold them at the angle necessary to allow the pine to grow straight. From this distortion, they encircle the pine gracefully. The two trees do not touch, except at one point where the thrust of the beech's growth has been turned at a direct right angle. But this touch in no way bends the pine's erect trunk, which springs in one rigid line from the earth and disappears into the beech's foliage.

Is this what closeness inevitably involves? The single oak tree in the open field just east of Avonlea spreads in a glistening, dancing summer freedom and reveals in winter the thrusting supports of this brilliance. The full stretch of its power declares itself totally achieved. When I was a child, its perfect growth encouraged and heartened me. It was a plain example of what a tree could be when given a chance. And the chance seemed mostly to be one of place: The acorn had rooted in rich soil, in an open space, in a latitude and longitude that favored acorns.

Yet between the pine and the beech there is a tension that has beauty too. The adaptation of the beech has the grace of submission to circumstances, and their conquest also, as its leaves glitter in the windy sunshine above a certain height and lend their delicate variety to the pine's harsh needles.

Every place is right for whatever is in it. Acceptance is more understandable to me now than to the child I was. But if I were a tree, I would prefer to be the Avonlea oak.

Yesterday my body began to feel right. The sick fatigue isn't there anymore. I feel steady. This time I wasn't at all sure that my body would heal to vigor. Now I can begin to stockpile strength as I am stockpiling work. The protection of the regular routine—the studio hours, the silent days, the naps, the evening reading of Henry James and George Eliot and E. M. Forster, the delicious and balanced meals, the lack of responsibility—has cradled me, and I am recovering from last winter.

31 JULY

A group of resident poets read their work last night in the living room of West House. They read in sequence, a man's voice, a woman's voice, each a poem, sometimes quietly repeated until it had settled into us all.

The pain of poets seems to me unmitigated. They are denied the physical activity of studio work, which in itself makes a supportive context for thought and feeling. In my twenties, when I was writing poetry steadily, I heard words at a high pitch. On the deep, full notes of three-dimensional form, demanding for its realization the physical commitment of my whole body, I floated into spaciousness. Using all my faculties, I could plumb deeper, without sinking forever.

Poetry was drawn out of my life, pulled out into lines. Sculpture is not. The works stand as I stand; they keep me company. I realize this clearly here because I miss them. I brought only table sculptures with me. In making my work, I make what comforts me and is home for me.

I expanded into love with the discipline of sculpture. Although my intellectual reason for abandoning writing for sculpture in 1948 was that I found myself uninterested in the sequence of events in time, I think now that it was this love that tipped the balance. Artists have no choice but to express their lives. They have only, and that not always, a choice of process. This process does not change the essential content of their work in art, which *can* only be their life. But in my own case the fact that I have to use my whole body in making my work seems to disperse my intensity in a way that suits me.

6 AUGUST

In skirting the role of the artist, I now begin to think that I have made too wide a curve, that I have deprived myself of a certain strength. Indeed, I am not sure that I can grow as an artist until I can bring myself to accept that I am one. This was not true, I think, before last winter. I was underground until the two retrospective exhibits of my work. Part of my intense discomfort this past year has been that I was pried out of my place there. I was attached to my secret burrow, which now begins to feel a little stale.

And also egotistic, confined, even imprisoning. I begin to see that by clinging to this position I was limiting what I had to handle in the world to what I could rationalize. As long as I stayed within my own definition of myself, I could control what I admitted into that definition. By insisting that I was "just me," I held myself aloof. Let others claim to be artists, I said to myself, holding my life separate and unique, beyond all definition but my own.

The course of events in my life has blasted this fortification, as it had blasted another in Japan. The fact of financial insecurity since my divorce in 1971, and the momentum of my own work and my efforts to be responsible for it, have thrown me into the open.

The open being: I am an artist. Even to write it makes me feel deeply uneasy. I am, I feel, not good enough to be an artist. And this leads me to wonder whether my distaste for the inflated social definition of the artist is not an inverse reflection of secret pride. Have I haughtily rejected the inflation on the outside while entertaining it on the inside? In my passion for learning how to make true for others what I felt to be true for myself (and I cannot remember, except very, very early on, ever not having had this passion), I think I may have fallen into idolatry of those who were able to communicate this way. Artists. So to think myself an artist was self-idolatry.

In a clear wind of the company of artists this summer, I am gently disarmed. We are artists because we are ourselves.

9 AUGUST

Aleksis Rannit is right: "Patience is the sister of mystery and tirelessness the best of roads." In this family, humility is the daughter of truth. As I work to understand my life, its scale seems to diminish, as a tree I gaze up into flattens when I walk up a mountain and look down on it. Humility is really more natural than pride, which seems to me always to involve a lie.

I remember when this lie began for me. I was in my mother's bedroom, standing in front of a gold-bordered pier glass. It was early afternoon. The light was sunny. It was warm.

I had on a white batiste undergarment, all one piece with a drop seat. The neck and arms were edged with narrow lace, and the same lace was on the ruffles gathered by elastic around my legs. I was being dressed for a party. My dress lay on the bed behind me, a translucent white cloud. My mother and my nurse were paying a new kind of attention to me, the same flavor of attention now paid to me at the openings of my exhibits. They were arranging my thin whitish blond hair into a "roach" curl, which was to run from the back of my head along its crown to the center of my forehead. They brushed my hair up, used a little water to hold it, and brushed again. The curl was totally artificial and had to be forced into being. Admonished to stand still, puzzled by their excited determination (very unlike the usual matter-of-fact tenor of the household), I addressed my image in the mirror.

I had never, to my recollection, seen myself before. I looked all right to myself in general; my feeling for my body seemed pretty well matched by what I saw. In fact, I was interested and would have been glad to have been left alone to look. But the chirps about the curl went on and on, and I began to feel uncomfortable. Something was being added to me. They wanted me to be more, and the "more" was the curl. I began to want the curl too, and I remember the first sick feeling of anxiety as they worked to get it to stick there. My healthy self felt whole without it, and recognized quite clearly that I was being made a fool of. But I was fascinated by being praised. The whole room danced with how cute I was. I knew I had done nothing except to stand there. I hadn't made the hair to begin with, much less the curl. But there it was; I began to want to please in order to get praise. I began to participate in the lie that I was something special, to take that role, to accept what I did not want and did not even think right for myself, in order to taste the sickly sweet flavor of praise.

I remember turning around from the mirror to the bed as they lifted the dress and held it out for me to step into. I held my head stiff with pride.

12 AUGUST

Unless we are very, very careful, we doom each other by holding onto images of one another based on preconceptions that are in turn based on indifference to what is other than ourselves. This indifference can be, in its extreme, a form of murder and seems to me a rather common phenomenon. We claim autonomy for ourselves and forget that in so doing we can fall into the tyranny of defining other people as we would like them to be. By focusing on what we choose to acknowledge in them, we impose an insidious control on them. I notice that I have to pay careful attention in order to listen to others with an openness that allows them to be as they are, or as they think themselves to be. The shutters of my mind habitually flip open and click shut, and these little snaps form into patterns I arrange for myself. The opposite of this inattention is love, is the honoring of others in a way that grants them the grace of their own autonomy and allows mutual discovery.

13 AUGUST

The roach curl is the earliest remembered strand of a web I wove to add on to what I was, what others wanted me to be.

The idea that I must meet arbitrary requirements caught fire from my clear recognition that I was very small and powerless; and it coalesced into the fear that if I failed to meet these mysterious requirements I would be abandoned. I began to watch. Anxiety sharpened my wits. From there, it was in retrospect only a step to my adoption of my mother's constructions for handling experience.

And even these I had to mistrust from the morning I trotted into the kitchen on my very short legs and found her sobbing on a stool behind the swinging door, wiping her eyes on the roller towel. I put my head in her lap and my arms as far around her as I could and pulled. She was like me. Of course, disciplined as always, she stopped crying, reassured me gently but a little briskly, gave me a cookie, and sent me to the garden again. But the fissure had opened, and I was more on my own than before. I understood that there was no safety. It would behoove me to grow up as fast as possible so that I could look after myself. And look after others too, for in that moment I had felt my mother's acceptance of comfort, her reliance on me. It was ambiguous, this reliance, because I knew and she knew that I could no more protect her than she, it had suddenly become clear, could protect me. But compassion is one of the purest springs of love, and it was love that I took with my cookie out into the garden.

14 AUGUST

The lives we lead appear, on logical examination, to result from the inexorable operation of cause and effect. The point at which we seem able to bring to bear our modicum of will is on our own attitudes, which then manifest themselves in the way we handle events. By our means we can try to tailor our ends. In the interval between event and responsive action, attitude acts like the chemicals in the nerve synapse, mediating the quality of the response. I try to work on my attitude toward what happens. In order to do this I find I must attempt to keep a distance, a position from which to examine my experience. For me, the key to this distance is the memory of how I was when I was very young. From this pure feeling of "I-ness," my life appears in retrospect to have been structured by a process of acquisition. I learned and retained and organized a set of facades appropriate to various occasions. When I encountered Gurdjieff's definition of personality as a compendium of many "I's," as distinct from the pure feeling of "I" with which we are born, which he calls "essence," I recognized its validity in my own experience.

15 AUGUST

Opinions underpin attitudes. When I began to move out of childhood, opinions, strongly expressed, seemed to me the hallmarks of adulthood. Choices had to be made between this and that, this being scorned, that being lavishly admired. Everything had to be judged, from trivialities to poetry. By these judgments you were yourself judged. I had acquired the roach curl by others' efforts, but later acquisitions had a more robust flavor; I flattered myself that I had made them for myself, rarely noticing how deftly I had tailored them to suit the fashion and how anxiously I had watched for reactions to them. Always a little behind, running to catch up, I panted to stay on the right side of all the good-bad dichotomies into which, it seemed, everything was divided. Choices, choices, choices. Did the violet scarf look right with the pink dress? Was it too cold to swim? What did so-and-so mean when she made such-and-such a remark? Why didn't Miss Perry marry Mr. Lockhart, who sat in the sun outside his hardware store all day? And I could make people laugh by saying, "Because he's too fat," tickling myself with pleasure while feeling sick because I never passed him without feeling deep compassion, so short on his little stool, so round a cannonball of stomach resting on his patiently parted knees. Why doesn't she marry him, I asked myself in a different part of myself, feeling the sere waste of their lives, his resignation to his lonely stool, hers to her sewing machine and to her stolid, passive mother.

The judgments I copied, then learned to make as I observed others make them, with just enough of myself in them to make them amusing or interesting contributions to conversation, began as fragments. It took time and effort to make them fit into cohesive plaques of personality that would be hailed with little cries of recognition and appreciation. It was a lot more difficult than the curl, but the effect was the same: I had to hold myself stiff, but I got the praise. And saved myself from being outcast.

16 AUGUST

The mist muffled sound early this morning. Very faintly, I heard footsteps on the gravel outside my turret. Just so do I remember my father's step, somewhere around the edge of my life when I was a child, never very far away, a little rushed, like a lively rabbit who was curious. He was an immensely loveable man who never managed to grip the ground in life. He inherited some money and never worked steadily except for charitable organizations and in occasional occupations. The youngest of six children, brought up in a large, rambling, gray clapboard house in St. Louis, he seemed to skim along from day to day, amused (for the most part) and cheerful. Spasmodically gripped by a desire to be, say, a writer or a painter, he would undertake lessons, write or paint for a while, and then the effort would dwindle into the preemptive course of events. Alternating with these spasmodic attempts to express himself were periods of depression during which he would drink. During these times, he wept slow tears that made his soft cheeks shine. My mother was incapable of understanding what he was suffering, and she dealt with him as she would have dealt with a disappointing child: She was polite and a little remote and ashamed.

It was to my mother that I turned for structure and for intelligent decision, but it was my father who matched my zest for life itself; everything that happened was a matter of curiosity to be explored and examined with hearty directness.

His recurrent lapses into alcoholic depression brought me smack up against the problem of loving someone whom I couldn't entirely respect. I chose to love him anyway and left understanding to fall into place later. This early choice has persisted. It is easy for me to love, to hold someone in affectionate confirmation, even when I can see quite plainly that the feeling is quixotic.

I have always been mystified by the speed with which people condemn one another. Feeling as righteous as Christ chastising the money-changers in the temple, they cast their fellows into the outer darkness of their disapproval. This seems to give them intense pleasure. Whenever I am tempted by this pleasure, I remember some impulse in myself that could have led me, granted certain circumstances, into the condemned position. This has caused me to distrust the part of myself that would relish self-righteousness.

17 AUGUST

This morning, for the first time since the afternoon of the opening last April, I reread the catalogue for my retrospective exhibit at the Corcoran Gallery of Art. The sick feeling of involvement with my work is definitely fading out. What I am left with is gratitude for all the effort so many people made for my work, and the beginning of an acceptance that allows me to let last year slip into the past.

19 AUGUST

Wood is haunting me. In 1961, I thought of making bare, unpainted wooden sculptures for the outdoors. On the National Cathedral grounds in Washington there is a carved wooden bench honed to honey color by weather. It stands under a tree, and so could a sculpture; this was my thought last spring as I ran my fingers over the pure, bare surface of the bench. I have been thinking about Japanese wood and the heavenly order of humble materials.

I come to the point of using steel, and simply cannot. It's like the marriage proposal of a perfectly eligible man who just isn't loveable. It is wood I love.

So any outdoor works, if they materialize, will not be heroic contemporary sculptures in the current tradition of David Smith. They will disintegrate in time at something comparable to the rate at which we human beings disintegrate, and with the same obvious subjection to its effects. They will not pretend to stand above the human span, but they won't be quite as short-lived. They may outlive several generations.

All my sculptures have these qualities, inherent in wood itself. Placing them outdoors would simply shift the balance of power into the hands of time.

21 AUGUST

I sometimes wonder whether my concern in my work with the limen of consciousness, with the threshold at which experience becomes just perceptible, is not related to my very long memory, which stretches back into my infancy. I remember lying on a table in the pale light of night. My lower body is drenched. My diaper is being changed. I already know that I will be comfortable very soon, and I feel patient. My nurse is tall and slender and serene, like my mother, though I know that she is not my mother. I trust her. Her hands are gentle and sure. Suddenly, from my right, a white shadow (flung up, I now suppose, by a passing automobile) lances across my vision, a deliberate lightning, illuminating progressively the windows, the slanted ceiling, my nurse's leaning form, my body, and a pile of cloth on the table beside me. I am totally surprised to find myself in a small, pulpy body in a place where light moves across darkness.

My nurse's name was Stella. She was beautiful, her skin a soft, pale copper underlaid with apricot. By the time my twin sisters were born, eighteen months after me, Stella had left us, and my mother took me to see her one warm afternoon. We walked down to Stella's house and found her lying on a pallet on the floor of the front room. Her length, so often measured vertically from my low perspective, was now shockingly horizontal. My knees were above her head. Her frail body was flat, scarcely lifting the cover under which it was neatly stretched, and her long hair, usually wound around her head, was combed out and spread thinly on the sheet. Her face was pure, as I had always remembered it, but now filmed with sweat. My mother, the same slender shape erect, stood with me, and we spoke quietly for a few minutes. Stella and I yearned for one another, but I could not stay. On the way home, my mother explained that she was dying, and managed by her own acceptance of love and parting to leave Stella whole and forever alive in my heart. There she remains fixed, intact, a touchstone for the quality of love. But love is too heavy a word for this light unity, the color and texture of honey, the sound of summer meadows in fresh winds.

23 AUGUST

I leave Yaddo this morning. It is raining steadily and the mist divides the trees outside my windows into stage flats. My finished work is packed into my car, which rides low with the weight. I arrived at Yaddo depleted; I leave fortified.

WASHINGTON, D.C.

AUGUST 1974 –JUNE 1975

26 AUGUST

My house is coming back under my hand. Clothes, washed and ironed, are hung in order in our closets. Sheets are piled up in crisp folds. Tables have been polished so that we may sit around them and laugh and eat a lot of the things we particularly like. The web of the house is caught up here and there, reattached, realigned, loosened, straightened. My bedroom curtains, lightly starched, dance with light. The front porch is swept ready for the winter firewood. Our cat, Rosie, curls around us in welcome, and Bear, our new puppy, guards us. He is charming, all out of proportion: enormous paws, long tail hanging off the end of his skinny body, heavy head with prune-colored eyes that follow us around when he himself is not gamboling under our feet.

2 SEPTEMBER

The stark fact of financial insecurity is once again stage center. Confronted by it in the summer of 1973, I circled the territory of my competence. Several alternatives presented themselves, only to be disqualified. I had one year of formal training in art, no degree. Teaching, requiring in the ordinary run of positions at least a master's degree in fine arts, would have meant further study, and this seemed ridiculously out of proportion, in addition to costing money itself. My B.A. and three years of professional experience in psychology were negligible professional equipment. A routine job remained a possibility, but one of last resort.

So I came then to the decision to ride out the jeopardy of art with as much courage and faith as I could. Turning it over once again now in my mind, I reach the same decision but with a change in attitude. Last year I did not have enough faith to trust myself to the course of events without a certain anxious steering toward success. Not for the glory of it, heaven knows, but for the sheer earning of money for the children and myself. I feel differently this year. I have set my sails without a preconceived course. It is a change to have sails to set. The metaphor is different. Last year a canoe, this year a ship in full sailing trim, keel stripped, lines coiled, sails patched with new cloth. My hand is light on the wheel. I am open to shifting winds and seas. I am even curious.

And can afford to be. My house is stout and my studio stands a few feet away from it in my garden. My children are healthy. Alexandra has her own apartment. Mary and Sam are well established in good schools and live here comfortably with me. Though I have little ready money, I am fortunate to have a modest inheritance, which backs me up.

Last winter, during the course of preparation for the retrospectives, I found myself on the crest of an unspeakable loneliness. Stopped, I told my children that I would like a day to myself and went to the National Gallery. I arrived just before the doors opened and waited on the steps leading up from the Mall, sitting patiently as in a doctor's waiting room. Admitted, I went straight to the Rembrandt self-portrait, painted when he was fifty-three, my age. He looked straight out at me, and I looked straight in at him.

There is a sort of shame in naked pain. I used to see it in my patients when I was working in psychology and nursing. They found it more seemly, more expedient to pull over themselves thin coverlets of talk. There is wisdom in this, an unselfish honor in bearing one's burdens silently. But Rembrandt found a higher good worth the risk and painted himself as he knew himself, human beyond reprieve. He looks out from this position, without self-pity and without flourish, and lends me strength.

I sat for a long while in one of the rectangular courtyards listening to the fountain. Feeling the artists all around me, I slowly took an unassuming place (for two of my own sculptures were somewhere in the museum) among the people whose lives, as all lives do, had been distilled into objects that outlasted them. Quilts, pincushions, chairs, tables, houses, sculptures, paintings, tilled and retilled fields, gardens, poems—all of validity and integrity. Like earthworms, whose lives are spent making more earth, we human beings also spend ourselves into the physical. A few of us leave behind objects judged, at least temporarily, worthy of preservation by the culture into which we were born. The process is, however, the same for us all. Ordered into the physical, in time we leave the physical, and leave behind us what we have made in the physical.

I went from the courtyard to Cézanne. Behind the paint marks, shining through like a promise, another reality transcends the tangibility of his paintings. Cézanne affirms that this world exemplifies, illustrates, hints. But he too was caught by his humanness. He died watching the door through which he hoped his son would arrive.

5 SEPTEMBER

An operation for a ruptured appendix in the autumn of 1938, my first year at Bryn Mawr College, temporarily ended my formal education; the surgeon refused to allow me to return for the completion of the year. The following summer I took a course of exercises with the psychiatric patients of Highland Hospital in Asheville, North Carolina, where we had moved from Easton, Maryland, when I was fourteen. These exercises, it was hoped, would strengthen my torn abdominal muscles. They served a more important function. I worked side by side with psychotic and psychoneurotic patients for two and a half hours every day, and slowly my inclination to be a psychologist hardened into determination.

"The schizophrenic patients don't suffer," I was told briskly. "They are happy in a world of their own." I did not think so. I watched their agony. Sometimes all would go well. Their arms and legs would coordinate, the volley ball would soar over the net, the push-ups would proceed rhythmically. Then a terrible pause would intercept their attention. Their bodies would freeze into a grotesque game of Statues. An attendant would coax them back into routine. Heartbreaking resignation stared from their eyes. They were doing the best they could. Their behavior, jerked by the automatic operation of a too idiosyncratic rationale, was logical only within its own context.

7 SEPTEMBER

Flush with youthful idealism and vigor, I set about to train myself. In people who were mentally ill, I found the pain I felt to be general so focused, so concentrated, that I could set myself against it. The practice of psychology offered me a position from which I could engage in battle.

Seven years later, in the spring of 1946, I abandoned the field.

It was not a retreat. I simply walked off it, quite unexpectedly. One minute I was relaxed behind my desk in the psychiatric laboratory at Massachusetts General Hospital in Boston, routinely giving psychological tests to a patient, and the next I was erect with the conviction that I was in the wrong place. The patient was a man in his early forties. He was on the psychiatric ward because the doctors thought his ulcer problem was more than usually complicated by psychological factors. Clad in a wretchedly worn, gray terry bathrobe provided by the hospital, bare-legged in floppy slippers, he sat on a straight chair in the center of a laboratory room lit by one bare hanging bulb. It was late in the afternoon, almost twilight. Around him was a detachment unusual in patients, who commonly had a song to sing, a tale to tell, a point to make. This man simply presented himself for examination. I remember feeling particularly competent, at ease in my white laboratory coat behind my desk, pencils at the ready. By this time, I had given these tests often, and the routine stretched blandly before me. I felt intact, invulnerable. A large window at my back gave me further advantage. The room and the patient were at my command. I was twenty-four.

I started with the usual questions in the usual soft, reassuring way. He answered neutrally. I remember noting "little emotional tone." I kept the introduction going for a while, hoping he would liven up. When he didn't, I was forced by the exigency of my own schedule to introduce the requirements of the test. This was the pivotal point: He had taken control by his passivity. I had to give him the test. He was granting me the grace to act upon him. I felt nonplussed, but continued. And then, as I paused at the end of the introductory instruction, he suddenly reared his head back and looked up at the hanging bulb with utter, unrelievable, acquiescent weariness, without hope.

The whole situation flashed into a lie. I saw myself as cardboard, propped up in an emblematic white coat behind a desk, irrelevant to his suffering. I realized instantly that my position was false. And shamefully impertinent—looking out from a stuck-up place while his legs stuck out naked. As long as I was separate from the man, I was useless to him. And beyond that opened the blinding insight that this uselessness undercut the whole structure of my endeavor for the past seven years.

It was over in that second when his head flung up against the light. I left Massachusetts General Hospital very soon thereafter. I thought it over, of course. I could have persisted and gone to medical school, become a doctor, and returned to do battle on a sounder and possibly more effective level of knowledge. But the basic separation remained an iron obstacle. No matter how much knowledge I could bring to bear, I would be in the position of acting upon other people, and always ultimately vulnerable to their acquiescence. They would control the amount of help they would allow me to give them. My skill would have to be pitted against those parts of them that wanted to remain ill. I had no stomach for this battle.

I was even more deeply appalled by the sudden realization that, if I locked myself into a position of having to be right for others, I might not only have to defend it, but also—dangerously—have to come to believe it myself.

These reflections were in no sense generalizations, only the tracks of my circling of my own situation and character. They had for me the slightly stale flavor that marks all afterthoughts. The truth of an intuitive leap is pure and straight. I had simply seen that I must unite with pain, abandon my artificial position of elevated immunity, in order to place myself in the way of assuaging it. The relationship of psychologist to patient had ceased to serve my purpose.

10 SEPTEMBER

The familiar strain of sustaining the various demands of daily life is once again a whine in the back of my mind. As I move from cleaning the house to washing and ironing to cooking to work in the studio to helping the children with their homework, even in the atmosphere of satisfaction these activities evoke, their inexorable sequence jerks my body into a faster pattern of response than is natural to it.

I could lower my standards but in so doing would sink with them, taking my children with me. It is not necessary for us to have candlelit dinners every night. But the ceremony of meals has always been important to regard. Where else can children learn so easily and pleasantly, and at such range when guests are included, what it is to be grown-up? The world of children is fascinating but very personal. The presence of adults in the full cry of conversation, with opinions, interests, engagements, and responsibilities discussed, crisscrossed by agreements and disagreements, laced with rhetoric, is so pungent with variety that children can learn without harm to their self-respect that they are, for all their interest to themselves, on their way to larger definitions.

Doing my duty as well as I can is essentially self-serving. It is only by attending to tasks and responsibilities as they arise that I can prevent myself from feeling angry that I cannot work in the studio as much as I want to. This is particularly true now, fresh as I am from the time at Yaddo when I was free from all demands other than those I made of myself. Anger at once excites and deadens my mind. The only answer to it I have found is efficiency. So I have tried to train myself always to keep abreast of the household routine in order to set myself free for clear concentration in the studio.

The decision to leave psychological work was the second major decision I made entirely on my own as an adult. Both seem to have been based on the same pattern: while pursuing a course of action apparently wholeheartedly, I had changed behind my own back.

When I applied to Yale in the spring of 1943, immediately before my graduation from Bryn Mawr, I was entirely convinced that I wished to pursue the graduate study of psychology. But when I received word from the university that I had been accepted, I was surprised to find myself mysteriously reluctant. I went for a walk to think things out. As if to invoke the presence of my mother, who had been dead for almost two years, I followed the path she used to walk and rested at a spot from which we had often gazed across the lake. As I sat looking at the landscape, I began to realize that my personal experience felt more valuable to me than my academic training. I had been working as a Red Cross nurse's aide during the summer following my graduation, and the care of the patients, mostly poor mountain folk, had opened my eyes to a whole new range of human life as well as to the satisfactions of using my hands. The more I turned it over in my mind, the more clearly I saw that what I wanted was a personal involvement with people rather than theoretical knowledge. By the time I got up off the grass, I had decided to join my two sisters in Boston, a city about which I was curious anyway because my mother and her family for generations before her had been born there. I would get a job, I decided, follow my life as it opened in front of me, and learn as I went along.

The decision to leave psychology was more dramatic because I came to it so suddenly, but the facts behind it fell into the same pattern. While working on research projects as a psychologist at Massachusetts General Hospital, I had also worked there at night as a nurse's aide, and my feeling for the poignancy of human lives had been deepened more by this personal service than by the work in the psychiatric laboratory. In addition, released from the discipline of college, I had read widely and with passion and had begun to write poetry and short stories. These two lines of development had slowly, and without my noticing what was happening, become my principal preoccupations both intellectually and emotionally. The more I observed the range of human existence—and I was steeped in pain during those war years when we had combat fatigue patients in the psychiatric laboratory by day and I had anguished patients under my hands by night—the less convinced I became that I wished to restrict my own range to the perpetuation of what psychologists would call "normal." And in the light of what I was reading—D. H. Lawrence, Henry James, T. S. Eliot, Dylan Thomas, James Joyce, Virginia Woolf—I had begun to see that my natural sympathies lay with people who are unusual rather than usual.

I honestly do not believe that I would be an artist now had I not been first a nurse's aide. The evening hours are poignant for hospital patients. In the gathering night, I rubbed backs, fetched ice water, washed faces and hands, remade beds to smooth comfort, toted bedpans, fed blind patients, gave babies their bottles, combed hair, moved patients from floor to floor, and occasionally helped in the emergency room. I listened to low voices, harsh voices, screams and sobs, looked at pictures of families, reassured frightened patients and their relatives, prayed, washed dying bodies to make their transit decent.

Finally night would fall over the lined-up beds. We would dim the lights one by one, patting and smoothing as we passed. Care made a kind of family. When I walked through the dark streets to the subway to return home, I used to feel them all behind me, as if I were myself stretched out inside each one.

So the ulcer patient who flung back his head crystallized for me a whole complex of personal emotional knowledge. I had begun, without realizing it, to open up the ducts through which my life would flow into art.

The hallmark of a decision in line with one's inner development is a feeling of having laid down a burden and picked up a more natural responsibility. By 1947, when I married James Truitt and moved to Washington, D.C., I had formed the habit of working on my own and had stockpiled a fair number of poems and short stories.

18 SEPTEMBER

I did not see a painting of high quality until I was thirteen. One hot afternoon, my father took my sisters and me to a friend's house to swim. We were led through a wide central hall at the end of which a screen door opened out onto a sunny lawn bordering a broad river. On the left of this door hung a small painting, the head of a girl in brilliant, clear colors. I gazed, transfixed. I remember swiftly calculating whether it would be rude to ask about it. I felt shy to thrust my curiosity forward, but I was blocking the way as I stood in front of it and I finally found it less awkward to ask who had made it. "Renoir," was the answer, "a French painter." Pressed by our small group, I moved on, but I have remembered the radiance of that little painting ever since, along with the dazzling insight that such beauty could be *made*.

Now, when I am called upon to look critically at the work of another artist, I watch for this response—the spontaneous rise of my whole being.

This instantaneous recognition of quality has been very, very rare in my experience with artists I am called upon to gauge, and in these modest circumstances I make it a habit to start by coming to respectful attention. It is such an act of courage to put pencil to paper that I begin by honoring the artist's intention.

Usually the work falls into a range I have to examine with my mind, in the light of what I know about the history of art and about its techniques. If the work is the result of honest effort, I acknowledge its validity but I look for the skill and talent that set apart potentially significant art. I try to discern the range of the artist's gift. When this range coincides with contemporary artistic concerns, the work has cogency in an historical context. This seems to me to be a matter of luck. A perfectly articulated range of sensibility may be just plain irrelevant to the problems confronting artists ambitious to make work of the highest quality in this historical sense. The degree to which an artist addresses these problems usually indicates the degree of his or her ambition. There is a sort of "feel" that marks relevant art. To some extent it can be learned, and here I find that young artists can badly deceive themselves: They can fall into using intelligence the wrong way; they can fail to realize that the purpose of scanning contemporary art is to use its articulations for the purer realization of their own work. As a carpenter might reach out for a newly invented saw, the work of other artists may suggest techniques or even solutions. But the essential struggle is private and bears no relation to anyone else's. It is of necessity a solitary and lonely endeavor to explore one's own sensibility, to discover how it works and to implement honestly its manifestations.

It is ultimately character that underwrites art. The quality of art can only reflect the quality and range of a person's sensitivity, intellect, perception, and experience. If I find an artist homing in on himself or herself, I bring maximum warmth to bear, knowing full well that the process is painful and, lonely as it is, susceptible to encouragement. Companionship helps. And the pleasure of being with younger or less experienced artists can be intense—the delight of watching people grow into themselves, becoming more than they have known that they are.

Sometimes artists use their work for ends that have nothing to do with art, placing it rather in the service of their ambitions for themselves in the world. This forces their higher parts to serve their lower parts in a sad inversion of values. And is, in art perhaps more than in any other profession, self-defeating. Purity of aspiration seems virtually prerequisite to genuine inspiration.

When I returned to Bryn Mawr in 1939 to continue my interrupted academic education, I dropped Latin, took the required course in philosophy, and came under the hand of Dr. Désiré Veltman. He burned into my brain the acid uncertainty of knowledge. A proposition examined became a proposition replaced by another proposition. Driven like Liza on the ice floes, I no sooner got my feet on one idea than I had to jump to another. I have always been grateful to him for allowing me to fall into the water often enough to gain some inkling of how to think without hardening the thought in the process of thinking it. He also taught me the pleasure of paradox: delight in Heraclitus's dictum that the only unchanging principle in life is that everything is always changing. The concept of the *logos* and the flux lying along a curved line that is at once convex and concave and unifies opposite forces in one identity has remained a spine as intimate to my thought as my backbone is to my body.

Later I studied Greek literature in translation. Of all the courses I ever took, it was the one closest to my bone. Looking back, I wonder why I stuck so tenaciously to my major in psychology, though I am glad I did. The discipline was incomparable: In one course we had eight hours of lab work a week and wrote a report on each experiment, one a week, which often ran to ninety-odd pages. It was difficult material and had to be learned on its own terms. I addressed myself to it as to battle, determined to master it. But a hard loneliness I had not known I had in me melted in the companionship of the Greeks. I embraced them. In some part of my mind Prometheus never leaves his chains; his vulture is my vulture. I flee the Eumenides. Aegisthus's horror is my horror. Clytemnestra's fires leap from headland to headland in the velvety night. Sappho's flowers burn pure color. Themistocles is forever throwing away his sword in a Thracian wood; dolphins scarcely more solid than the pewter sea surge around him. Odysseus fends and feints around the wine-dark Mediterranean, scratching in muscular perplexity and arching his charms. Achilles cannot help killing Hector, whose great bronze helmet rolls under the walls of Troy from which his son Astyanax, forever catching his breath, is flung to the ground. Andromache's pain detonates off Cassandra's piercing syllables. The sandals of Tiresias lift stately puffs of dust. His blind eyes comfort Oedipus, whom I follow to Colonus.

The Greek poets saw and felt, and then wrote. They learned from suffering, and the way they learned was to make the effort to articulate their personal experience into forms that transcended it. They combined examined experience with the discipline of art to bring forth a statement forever useful to their fellow human beings. It was their solution to the problem of universal pain that struck me: not the direct alleviation, which I was pursuing so hotly in my study of psychology, but a way that beckoned people toward aspiration.

22 SEPTEMBER

Biology stretched physical scale. Under the microscope, largeness became smallness, which became largeness. It was obvious that both ends were open on this continuum.

I found myself able—I was totally astonished—to draw. With a very sharp pencil, I outlined a beautifully intact amoeba and placed the nucleus where I saw it. It was my first taste of picking up and moving into visual terms what I saw to be true. Being stuck in my habit of literary expression, I had never thought of this possibility as a personal option before, and never actually thought of it then, just delighted in the balanced coordination of eye and hand. The paramecium was a real field of action; the placement of the cilia had to be invented, their movement being too rapid for exact depiction. I remember memorizing the length and generalizing the nature of the pattern their motions made so I could, in terms of art, abstract them accurately. I kept my pencil very, very sharp. I made the lines lightly, but firmly, bearing down just enough. Absorbed by the incredibly compelling life I saw under the microscope, my pencil was in its service. Given a dogfish laid out on a tray, I traced his nervous system with passionate concentration. Palms wet with my intent to see it all, I kept losing the tiny threads and then asking for help. Relocated, I tracked them relentlessly. Under my pencil, the lines *were* this struggle.

And, when I came to the dissection of a lobster, I connected this line with life and death. Mine was brought to me alive, his heart injected with dye so I could trace his blood's circulation. When I had finished, I took my tray to the instructor, who killed my lobster and handed him back to me to dissect further. His life ended under my pencil, and continued in my pencil.

The range of simple biological fact was presented in such perfect order and with such ardor for scrupulous methods of investigation that my whole understanding developed soundly. I was given a kind of map, like one of those plastic sheets that, placed over jumbled lines, startlingly organize them into a readable picture. This order fleshed out my inherent intuition of order; it strengthened the conviction that I could trust my own being.

And the discipline of laboratory work placed a pencil in my hand and demanded that through it I convey what I experienced. This cut the first direct channel between my experience and my hand.

23 SEPTEMBER

My mother was a friend of probity. She guarded the ramparts of my integrity. Girded with love, she patrolled the byways of my character. When she spoke, I listened with particular trust, knowing that, although I might not like what she said, I would learn. I trusted her honor to guard mine, having caught its spirit on my torch. When she died, I felt the spring of release from this watchfulness. It was the most irreplaceable bereavement.

She only betrayed me once. In the fall of 1939, when I was confidently expecting to return to Bryn Mawr for the freshman year that had been interrupted by appendicitis, she invited me for a walk. As we rounded a corner near our house, she announced that my twin sisters needed educating and she could not afford to send me back to Bryn Mawr, having forfeited a whole year's tuition when I had been unable to return the previous November. She continued to say that she had written Bryn Mawr to this effect and had enrolled me in Duke University. I remember standing in the middle of the road, stunned. I simply could not take in the fact that she could have snatched so wantonly away from me what I knew to be my salvation—the opportunity for excellence. I asked quick questions. Did my father know? Yes. Was the whole matter settled? Yes. Was there any option? No. Had she definitely, irrevocably, decided? Yes. She stood there, confronting me in her impeccable white sneakers, and I felt the iron of her decision. I cried and begged and groveled and for the first time in my life felt the limits of my own control over myself. She not only could control my life, she intended to do so, sharp against my will and my own feeling for myself. I had visited a friend at a large university like Duke and had been appalled by the crowded quarters in which my friend lived with three roommates, by the giggling, the disorder, the heavy bodies, the hundreds of herded students, the indifference of a population leveled by sheer numbers into what I at that time felt to be mediocrity. In a blinding, terrified flash, I saw that I was to be placed in that situation, forced to adjust beyond my sensibility. Crying did no good. She held her ground. We returned to the house, having got no further than the curve of the road.

Twenty-four hours later a letter arrived from Bryn Mawr offering me a full tuition scholarship. The dean of admissions, an austere and scholarly woman, had saved me. She must have made the decision by some intuition beyond my guessing. My record in the few weeks I had been in college had been in no way unusually good, and indeed I had failed a Latin test just before the Thanksgiving vacation during which I had been stricken by appendicitis. Partly, no doubt, she was motivated by a sense of fairness. But I felt, beyond that, a faith in me I will always remember with profound gratitude. My grandmother used to say that we never do other people good when we intend to. But we do, even if rarely.

24 SEPTEMBER

In my last year at Bryn Mawr I took creative writing with a professor who lent my work a most delicate attention. Her intellectual sensitivity, as translucently articulated as the frame of a praying mantis, led me to trust her skill; we took equal pleasure in elucidating my tales of my childhood insights. She taught me to be succinct, to weigh each word in my hand, and she clarified for me the syntax by means of which I could make transitions—one in particular I remember in which an ailing old judge totters up his shallow porch steps, lowers himself into his creaking wicker rocking chair, and leans over to speak down to the little girl who was myself, staring up at him from the street.

She encouraged me to trust the landscape of my childhood, radiantly preserved in my memory. And it was to this source that I returned in November 1961.

26 SEPTEMBER

I find myself at an impasse. I have no money to make more sculpture and am hard put to pay for the fabrications now in the studio.

I met the same obstacle when the Corcoran Gallery

Workshop, in which I had been working for some months since my separation from my husband early in 1969, unexpectedly closed. I had no studio, no money to rent one, and no money to make sculpture anyway.

My first reaction was to hurry. I stretched myself to finish *Elixir*. I rushed around in an effort to find, even without knowing how I was going to pay for it, another place to work. Like a chicken with its head chopped off, I flopped frantically. One afternoon I was sweating on my ladder, moving swiftly up and down, hand held lightly to spread thin paint in yet another transparent coat, feeling the color deepen under the brush. Suddenly I stopped, climbed down, washed my brush, and went outside to sit on the front step and think. It was June, warm and sunny. I was very, very tired. My whole body hummed with fatigue and strain.

I remembered as I sat there the principle of reverse solution I had discovered on another hot summer day some years earlier when my children were very little. I had taken my three and two of their friends to Dumbarton Oaks Gardens, where we strolled around happily until the guards began to close the park; it then became apparent that Alexandra and her friend had disappeared, last seen running toward the rose garden. We called and called and finally returned home to find that Alexandra had asked a policeman to drive them back to our house. The fact that struck me, appalled by my own stupidity, was that she and her friend had gone through the gates ahead of us—and I had never thought of looking for them *outside* the garden. I had been stuck in my preconception that they must be inside because I had last seen them there. From that time forward, I had always tried to remember to reverse solutions when I sensed the sticking feeling that marked unintelligent behavior.

So as I sat on the step thinking, it occurred to me that I might regard being deprived of a studio as a present. I began to entertain the idea that, if I looked upon it as such, I could turn myself into it instead of away from it. By the time I got up from the step I had decided to close the studio, store my equipment in my basement and my unfinished work with my other work under Walter Hopps's aegis at the Corcoran Gallery of Art, and make drawings in my living room on the white table I had used to change the children on when they were babies. The clear, tranquil sanity of adjustment to reality floated me into peace of mind.

A Guggenheim fellowship, granted in April 1970, rescued me from restriction. With the foundation's permission, I used part of the funds to build a studio in my backyard.

The Chinese say that every man should plant a tree, write a book, and have a son. And build a building. At my white table in the living room, I made a rough scale drawing of what I wanted the studio to look like and worked with an architect to build as large and as practical a structure as I could for as little money as possible. Chance helped us along. The slope of the garden places the southern windows almost flush with my lawn and allows a neighbor's trees to sketch a delicate tracery against the northern panes. The double doors leading into the alley are exactly the right height for a truck hoist so heavy sculptures can be moved in and out. Everything works. The heat is heavenly after years of working in cold buildings, and the water runs hot. The Tokyo chilblains have receded into memory, along with the Easter basket of painty bowls and brushes I used to carry home every evening from Twining Court, the dilapidated carriage house where I worked in the early sixties. It is a wonderful studio and in it, on the same white table, I can make drawings this winter.

Every narrow financial passage helps to prepare me for the next. Once, in 1969, having held out for weeks, I decided that at 1:30 p.m. I would telephone my financial counselor and ask for a loan on my small stock of securities. At 1:25 André Emmerich, my New York dealer, telephoned to say that a sculpture had been sold and he was not taking any commission. Since then the lilies of the field blow a little less stiffly in the chill wind.

A sort of stillness comes upon me. I feel the constriction of possibility, the limitation, almost physically, like elastic walls pressing on me and seeming to harden as the money dries up. The solution is the acceptance of immobility, and gratitude that faith just perceptibly withstands fear.

Actually, my financial situation is never as dire as I feel it to be against the background of the luxury in which I have been privileged to live, by the grace of my husband for twenty-one years and of my inheritance from my family— not enough to live on but a bulwark. My anxieties, such as my concern to provide my children with excellent educations, are indeed luxuries in themselves. They are sharpened, however, by the fact that I have continually to invest my financial capital in my work, essentially in myself, and then am forced to meet the responsibility of that investment if I am to maintain the standards I wish for my family. Yet, had I not so invested it steadily since 1961, I would have had no foundation from which even to consider the possibility of continuing my work when my divorce faced me with financial limitation.

I OCTOBER

In my junior year at Bryn Mawr, I took Renaissance art, in my senior year modern art, and entered into a kingdom in which I have reveled, like Matisse's dancers, ever since. The Greeks were closest to my bone, the artists to my heart and to a certain passion for technique that had been born in biological drawing. It interested me that inert material could be turned to the service of meaning. It still is a miracle to me that a pencil line, ipso facto a material mark, can have integral meaning. The Greek poets spoke. The artists placed, and their passion for placement echoed my own. My observation that placement in itself had meaning reinforced my intuitive conviction that Plato was right in thinking the material world a reflection of laws it serves to exemplify. Art, a human arrangement of matter, can throw bridges, at once fragile and imperative, between these areas of action. It can heighten our insight into the odd plight of having to live in a situation in which everything is relative to everything else. It objectifies a particular point of contact between human beings and matter, and strikes sparks in the very fact that a person has set a hand to arrange matter, has undertaken to be Promethean. Artists necessarily beckon the vulture.

And certain artists beckoned me. Giotto: a blue shape, another blue shape, gray—my heart was wrung. Another arrangement of color slightly different in proportion—my heart lifted. Color and form in themselves (I cannot say how deeply this caught me) had a meaning to which my whole being answered. The world I felt behind the world I fumbled with my senses was Piero della Francesca's kingdom: stripped, clarified, pure, more real than ordinary matter. If I lived in that limpid space, I thought to myself, I would be at home.

6 OCTOBER

Orion strides the southern sky once more in his autumn place. I go out into the early morning to see him, rising to his boldness. It is curious to me that people take straight lines for granted. We never see them unless we make them ourselves; even the apparently straight horizon of the ocean against the sky curves if we see it from the air. Orion's "belt" is three stars.

The line of the gravity holding us to the earth, plumb from the sky to the globe under our feet, is the given element from which we abstract the concept of straightness in our own personal experience.

7 OCTOBER

All told, I now have available about one hundred dollars in ready money. This is too low an ebb. Yesterday my heart pounded all day and my left eye is jumping and jerking. The struggle is to hold myself submissive to a process of diminishment. There is a point at which lack of money feels like a draining of bone marrow. I begin seriously to contemplate taking a routine job of some sort but am loath to do so. Not out of laziness but because I fear the kind of sickening failure implicit in betrayal of self, the spending of my energy drop by drop instead of into the waves that lift my work into existence.

8 OCTOBER

André Emmerich has once again come to my rescue. He has advanced me a sum on a prospective sale.

9 OCTOBER

I am sick again. The tension mounted yesterday, unbearably. I got everything ready for the children's dinner and went to bed. This morning I have a sore throat and a cold.

The insecurity drained me below my level of endurance. It is an interesting process to watch, and this time I did reasonably well, I think: my savings and then my daughter Mary's savings, which she sweetly lent me, and then eking from day to day, no bills owed except a recent one for $92.00, and all with a fair degree of equanimity. It's my habitual pattern to do all right in crises and then to have a reaction. The Yaddo sickness was like this. Each time the pattern repeats, the strings of my being seem stretched into further weakness. Or could it be that my sight is too short to see those strings that are strengthened? Perhaps it is a realignment of energy. I keep hoping to learn. But I get discouraged because I don't seem to have learned fast enough in the past to forfend the draining in the present.

One laboratory measure of sensitivity is a discrimination in acuity called a Just Noticeable Difference, J.N.D. for short. This time there was, fortunately, a J.N.D. in my degree of faith.

My limen of financial insecurity has been set high by my privileged life, but it is curious to me that the feeling of insecurity is for me a kind of violation, as if something violent were being done to me. I flop about in a dim parody of the first violence I ever knew.

I was eighteen months old when my twin sisters were born and the atmosphere of my life changed abruptly. I was moved to the second floor from the third-floor nursery and put out into the garden so I would be out of the way. After that I spent a good deal of time in the garden, alone.

Stretching west, the garden was long and narrow, divided at about three-quarters of its length by a row of Lombardy poplars beyond which was an area less carefully tended than the eighteenth-century boxwood and flower beds nearer the house. In this wilderness, where the vegetation was sometimes over my head, a wire fence ran along the south border. Through its metal links, I could see the whitewashed clapboard back wall of a shed housing the grocer's chickens. Violets grew profusely under its eaves. Nourished by chicken droppings, enormous, sweet-smelling blossoms burgeoned from thick-springing leaves.

The grocer would appear periodically in his white canvas apron and kill a chicken. Grasping its yellow legs in one hand, he would wrestle it into position on a stained stump and chop off its squawking head with a hatchet. As he did so, he would drop its legs and its body would flap and flop around in the sudden silence. Then he would pick it up, bloody neck dangling, and carry it off with casual power to be plucked in the back of his store across the street from our house. I used to stand with my fingers grasping the wire mesh of our fence and watch it all. With the plain eye of childhood, I realized that what I was seeing had to be taken for granted: violets in the foreground and off to the left the matter-of-fact wielding of death. The grocer purveyed provisions to my family. His wife was roly-poly and they were generous with oatmeal cookies kept in a glass jar on their counter.

When I was a little older, I was able to go to the other side of the fence and look at it all closely. The house next door on that side was, in the higgledy-piggledy of a small town, the undertaker's. His shades were always drawn right down to the sills, but at the back door there were galvanized garbage pails. I used occasionally to see fibrous rags soaked with blood and yellow pus, thrusting from under these bulging tin lids. Bracing myself, I would walk past them into the back lot to visit the chickens, at whom I would gaze in wonder, knowing what they didn't know. Once I took my mother some violets and, when she asked me where I had found such beautiful ones, answered evasively, vaguely conscious that this area of exploration had better be kept to myself. As far as I can remember, this was my first lie, told to keep intact for myself alone the truth of what I had seen with my own eyes, and to preserve my independence.

This winter is bringing me to a confrontation with the truths behind truths, like the color I know to lie just beyond color.

I remember how startled I was when, early in 1962, I realized that I was becoming obsessed with color as having meaning not only in counterpoint to the structures of fences and the bulks of weights—which were, I had thought, my primary concern—but also in itself, as holding meaning all on its own. As I worked along, making the sculptures as they appeared in my mind's eye, I slowly came to realize that what I was actually trying to do was to take paintings off the wall, to set color free in three dimensions for its own sake. This was analogous to my feeling for the freedom of my own body and my own being, as if in some mysterious way I felt myself to *be* color. This feeling grew steadily stronger until the setback of my experience in Japan when, in despair that my work no longer materialized somewhere in my head, I began to concentrate on the constructivist aspects of form, for me a kind of intellectual exercise. When we came back to America in 1967, I returned home to myself as well as to my country, abandoned all play with form for the austerity of the columnar structure, and let the color, which must have been gathering force within me somewhere, stream down over the columns on its own terms.

When I conceive a new sculpture, there is a magical period in which we seem to fall in love with one another. This explains to me why, when I was in Yaddo and deprived of my large pieces, I felt lonely with the same quality of loneliness I would feel for a missing lover. This mutual exchange is one of exploration on my part, and, it seems to me, on the sculpture's also. Its life is its own. I receive it. And after the sculpture stands free, finished, I have the feeling of "oh, it was *you*," akin to the feeling with which I always recognized my babies when I first saw them, having made their acquaintance before their birth. This feeling of recognition lasts only a second or two, but is my ample reward.

13 OCTOBER

Yet perhaps I can speak so austerely of this kind of reward because I fell so easily into place in the world outside my studio. I had met Kenneth Noland at the Institute of Contemporary Art, where I began my study of sculpture in 1948, and, when he saw what I was doing in 1962, he instantly began to help me in every possible way with the most complete generosity. He spoke of my work to David Smith and to Clement Greenberg, whom I already knew as friends; they came to my studio and encouraged me. And he introduced me to André Emmerich, his own dealer.

My connection with André Emmerich had indeed already begun, in a strange exchange that took place in 1953. He saw, and bought from the Baltimore Museum of Art Regional Show, my sculpture of a head. Just under life-size, polished blue-black cement with silver Sculpmetal laced into the interstices left by the casting process, the head is thrown back, the mouth open in a cry. The material, at once decorative and threatening, echoes, as it contains, this cry. I don't remember the piece as being totally successful, but something about it caught André Emmerich's eye and he bought it for $25; that would have been that had not a young couple in Baltimore already bought it, so it had to be returned, with the result that all record of it has been lost.

I met him for the first time in September 1962, when he came to Washington for Morris Louis's funeral. As we waited for the ceremony, he asked if he could come to my studio and then offered me a one-shot, trial show in February 1963. At the end of the opening of that exhibit, he simply turned to me and said, "I hope this is the first of many exhibits," and I have been with him ever since.

21 OCTOBER

I write this about 3:00 a.m., having just awakened from another of my repetitive dreams about the sea.

I stand on a firm reddish orangish purple beach. Behind me ramparts of blue-black slate rise straight into air that is only air, not sky, and is itself a blue-black slate color. I am with a man I deeply love, am one with. Our bodies are the same texture, at once lighter and more dense, more flexible and more fibrous than this body of mine now. We are the same tone as the beach and the cliffs and the sky, a dark purplish slate color. We have the endurance of metal infinitely inflected into lightness.

We look out from the beach onto a part of the sea we do not know. Our bodies match the sea and are only slightly more solid, hard as fish are hard with muscle, but alive all through like the sea. We are wary of the water because we are separate from it, but only slightly more so than from the beach, and that because we have to breathe. We run down the sloping sand, which rasps our soles, and move into the water. We are the same temperature as the water. Its purple folds our purple into itself, under and over. But we remain ourselves. We love one another so closely that each other is other only as much as we are other than the sea. The water is stronger than even we are accustomed to. I think fearfully that I cannot go through these waves, but I see that he is breasting them, and since our bodies are one substance I realize that I also must be stronger than I feel. Nonetheless, we both have in our minds the knowledge that the tide turns. We never forget our position off the slate cliffs.

We find ourselves very far out. We have decided to let the tide carry us. We have already noticed that the cliffs end off to our right where the water boils up into transparent mauve over shallow, orange rocks. The tide pulls us. It is too late to turn back and we do not want to anyway. Our spirits answer one another: We agree that we have a chance to live through and beyond. All the while the sea is pulling, pulling faster and faster. We move swiftly, borne on its current, which now turns us onto the mauve shoals. Our bodies whip and sing in the water's movements, which are the music of our own cells. Out of the crescendo we are pulled abruptly around into the lee of the cliffs. We are trembling with exhilaration. We have taken our chance once more, and once more we have survived. The magic begins to recede. The color is draining from the rocks, the water, our bodies. We are separating. We are conscious of each other. I begin to feel "I."

I am awake. Rosie is curled at my feet. My soft white woolen blanket is warm over me. I am here.

The dream's energy lasted all day yesterday. My animus, brave companion in adventure, remains with me.

I seem always to have known this companion in a way acceptable to myself as a woman—not, of course, under the title of "animus" but as a recognizable part of myself, reliable and useful. The direct line of Boston bluestockings immediately preceding me in the family history—my grandmother was in the first graduating class of Smith College; my mother graduated from Radcliffe—sanctioned my natural independence of mind, and has throughout my life rendered me comfortable with being a woman without having to be sewn into a stereotype.

My first recollection of being a girl is sunny and has to do with giving a present to my father, a little white box my mother hands to me while I stand in my crib and guides me to transfer to my father. He opens the box, smiles with delight, thanks me and my mother together as they lean over me and we all three hug. It is difficult to say exactly why I felt this to be a feminine thing to do. Perhaps I picked up my mother's welcome into a world in which women give to men. And something, too, in my father's response, a kind of expansiveness men tend to have with women and not with each other. In my memory I seem to know that my being a little girl enhanced the whole exchange. By this time I had somehow absorbed the knowledge that my body was like my mother's, that I would grow into that form, distinct from the form of my father. The fatal roach curl came later, but I was nudged into position for it by the assumptions, based on my sex, that adults made about me—another illumination of how actions can be taken to prove assumptions.

My implicit femininity was in all these aspects but was more than any of them, as the whole is always more than the sum of its parts. The essence remains ephemeral but distinct. I still feel it, recognize it. I am without it when I am alone if I make the effort to think very clearly; if I do not, it tinctures my thinking. I have learned to take it into consideration, in a sense to guard against it as a blurring factor, to try to remember that my sex is secondary to me, I separate from it.

24 OCTOBER

I opened my eyes a moment ago into the maple leaves outside my window. Almost simultaneously with the act of identifying them as these particular leaves and thus placing myself, I saw them as painting, an arrangement of values.

The other afternoon when I was entertaining my daughter Mary in her bath, she asked me whether I thought artists were "just born that way." I said I thought they might be. "How?" she asked. I said I didn't know, but that there was rarely a time when I wasn't half-consciously translating what was around me into terms of art, that as I stood at the door—for I was on my way out when this exchange took place—I had been absorbing her brown body against the white tub, the yellow top of the nail brush, the dark green shampoo bottle, Sam's blue towel, her orange towel, and could make a sculpture called *Mary in the Tub* if I ever chose to. These elements arranged themselves into proportions of color, the weights of which gave me the meaning of what I was seeing. Mary and I laughed, partly out of the pleasure of talking with one another and partly out of wry recognition of everyone's oddness.

"Is it just that my senses operate in this way?" I asked myself a moment ago when the leaves presented themselves not as objects but as values. Not entirely, obviously, but I do think that my marked nearsightedness has had a lot to do with my abstraction of what's around me.

It was not discovered until I was in the fifth grade that I was nearsighted, and part of my shock in moving from the tutorship of a governess into school was the abrupt realization—very frightening—that I was inadequate. I simply couldn't see the blackboard in the classroom and, having never before been obliged to see clearly at a distance, was at a loss to know what was wrong. I remember feeling sick (a pervasive malaise akin to depression), realizing that this was a new feeling and not knowing what to do about it because I couldn't immediately isolate the cause. I only knew that I couldn't do what the other children could, but, since they were competent in ways that were also new to me, I wasn't sure precisely what I was lacking.

As I remember, it took a couple of weeks for the teachers to find out what was wrong, why this apparently intelligent child was failing to understand what was going on around her. It was the history teacher, a practical woman who liked dates and facts, who caught on. She must have been surprised to discover a real disability in so carefully nurtured a child. It is really curious that no one had noticed before then. I remember my mother saying, "Children should be brought up like cabbages—lots of sun and space and let alone to grow," but it is only at this moment that I realize the extreme oddness of such an altogether privileged child being so neglected in so basic a way.

When I got my glasses, gold-rimmed and prim, to match my little yellow pigtails, I was astounded by detail. Leaves were particularly surprising, so distinct and so separate. I was catapulted into a wholly new world, as if I had been reborn. Everything had to be rethought. I remember going around and looking, checking out to see in the new way what I knew the old way. The thing that struck me was the clarity, the precision, the multiplicity of individuality. The world had always been an actively moving, enticing blur to me before, a sort of challenge I had to make sense of by guesswork because it presented itself as a mystery. I had always felt at a distance from it, and in truth that's the way my senses presented it to me: I saw at twenty feet what other people saw at three hundred. A whole world had been formed on the basis of faulty information.

The more I think about it, the more this fact seems to lie like a spine along which my early development was organized.

It must have operated to make me self-centered in the literal sense. I could only operate confidently within a short radius. This is still characteristic. What I feel, I feel intensely, but it has to come to me, within my ken, under my hand, for me truly to grapple with it. A kind of stubbornness, which may originally have been a defense against demands beyond my perceptive ability, resists the rush of sensory activity. I remember squatting down a lot as a child, examining everything close up. I remember feeling more at home inside my mind than outside it. It was always natural for me to make up images in my head. When my mother read to my sisters and me in the evening, the words made pictures that, now when I think of it, must have been clearer than what I actually saw with my eyes. This tendency to live inside my mind must have reenforced my adoption of my mother's way of constructing her world so matters would go the way she thought they should. She also was nearsighted, and my development may have matched hers for this reason among others. The world couldn't have been real to either of us the way it is to people who can see clearly. Indeed, I always have to make a psychological effort, which must have originally been a physical effort, to focus on it at all. My natural focus is interior.

When in the biology lab I saw the amoeba under the microscope, I now seem to recall recognizing not only the fluid thrust of the pseudopodia but also a change in focus akin to that which had once altered the whole world for me. This practice of changing focus has been a habit of my mind ever since. I play the scale of my experience up and down. My toe hurts: the pain throbs into a universe expanding and contracting. An ant's antenna flicks a leaf: a hurricane wind whips a palm frond. Observation is extrapolated into abstraction.

Perhaps the direct line between the amoeba and my pencil set up a connection made powerful by this reactivation of what had been so total a change in my life. The pencil, which fixed the line of the amoeba's fluid body, tapped this unconscious source of energy. This is speculation. But I do know that when I put a pencil on paper I feel that between the point and the paper there is a coming into being from a live source within myself.

It interests me that, had I not been born nearsighted, I would not now, as I age, be able to see as clearly to work. As it is, I can simply take off my glasses and everything close to my eyes is blissfully distinct. And I think too that, because I couldn't see, I was forced to develop my kinaesthetic senses to what may perhaps be an unusual acuity. When I heard that bats operate by radar, I knew instantly how they do it.

27 OCTOBER

It is not only nearsightedness that now appears to me to have been an advantage in the development of my life, but also the operation for appendicitis, which at the time seemed so catastrophic.

This advantage I owe to the mother of a beloved old friend, the only other adult in my childhood—with the exception of my father—whom I recognized as being as adventurous as I, equally willing to throw her hat over a windmill. It was her Christian Science principles that prevented her calling in a doctor when I fell ill under her roof while on my Thanksgiving vacation in my freshmen year at Bryn Mawr. My appendix ruptured, and I underwent an emergency operation at Johns Hopkins Hospital for acute pelvic peritonitis. She spun my life into a direct right angle. Not only did I lose the remainder of that year at college, being considered by the surgeon too weak to return, but also the infection prevented my conceiving a child until fate led me again to Johns Hopkins in 1955, when a courageous doctor was able to operate on me and enable me to bear children.

These are the exterior facts. It is the interior facts that point to the teleological way in which life operates.

First, I was too young for college in 1938, far more unhappy than I had realized, and not doing very well academically. The shock of stringent demands, so much more peremptory than those of my rather inadequate preparatory school, had unsettled me. By Thanksgiving vacation I was really in over my head. In the fall of 1939, when I returned to college, I was not only steady but also had firmly conceived the purpose of becoming a psychologist as a result of having been exposed to the psychiatric patients at Highland Hospital.

Secondly, I came very close to death. I was told afterward that, had the operation been three hours later, I would inevitably have died. I have never forgotten the full flood of peace on which I felt myself radiantly supported. My friend's mother had been correct in her faith. I was indeed held in love, and this knowledge became fact for me as it could have in no less critical way.

Thirdly, had I borne children during the first years of my marriage, as I yearned to do, I would not have been forced to concentrate on my own development. It was from 1948, the year following my marriage, until 1955, when Alexandra was born, that I developed the studio discipline that has supported my work ever since.

But my friend's mother's greatest gift to me was a legacy of ambition. Her intellectual curiosity, her élan, her gaiety, her ceaseless questioning and probing of experience all conspired to make the world open for me, subject to the fresh definition of my own mind, a domain for enterprise. She lived in an ambience of creativity. I don't think it ever occurred to my mother, the other dominant influence in my life as a child, to add anything to the world. Not so this friend. She was always adding. Her stance was active. It was from her that I picked up the value of forming opinions, and to her that I owe my first inkling that an enterprising life was available as a personal possibility.

29 OCTOBER

Restoration is one of the disciplines inherent in the vulnerability of my work. I used to be sick at heart to send sculptures out into the world as whole and pure as I could, only to see them return damaged. This is more routine now. The difficulty is that the surface of a heavy, large, freestanding structure is very hard to protect. Fortunately, acrylic paint is washable, but dents are troublesome to mend. There is, too, I think, a sort of resentment people can feel against an object arrogant enough to claim equal, or even greater, space than their own bodies. They sometimes kick a sculpture on purpose; or push it over, as someone did in the Corcoran Gallery of Art.

Another source of vulnerability is the stubbornness with which people meet an unfamiliar concept. Sculpture, theoretically, is strong, tough, durable, and falls into the category of objects to be handled more or less routinely. It is difficult to convey the idea that these structures are intrinsically paintings, as delicate of surface. They are troublesome. They make demands, which is not an attractive characteristic.

Restoration always confronts me with the dilemma of artists' identification with their work: When my sculptures are damaged, there is an inescapable feeling that *I* am damaged. Art is always an extension of self—how else could artists pour their power into it? Like amoebas, they put forth a form and flow into it. And like amoebas, they can submit to binary fission, at the end of which their work is separate from themselves. But it took me a while to realize that this final step was necessary. When I was a younger artist, I reveled in the marvel of identification: It is I.

I NOVEMBER

Last night I sat in my quiet living room with deep contentment. A light hand seemed to have touched each object, leaving it refreshed. Kenneth Noland's beautiful painting *Mandarin* echoed an order into which these familiar things have evolved over the years of community with one another. When Sam had finished his bath, I went upstairs to mine and to my peaceful dark bedroom, all open to the night wind.

The tangle of the last two months is unraveling. I marvel at the ease and speed with which events take place after such a blockage. Like brook water released from matted weeds, they positively gurgle.

The studio is moving in orderly fashion toward serenity as one finished sculpture after another stands free in its coat of glassine paper to await its future fate. The children and I thread smoothly in and out of one another, each on our appointed rounds in the winter routine. The garden is raked, forked, turned, and mulched, muted to dun, quiescent. A rhythmic exchange is making everything move easily. Every demand is met and matched by an appropriate energy. There seems to be nothing I can do to make this happen. I can only be alert to the current and make sure to ride it when it does happen.

2 NOVEMBER

In the last few months, I have become more conscious of how my work takes form. It sometimes happens unexpectedly. Just as I wake up, a series of three sculptures may present themselves somewhere that seems high over my head in my consciousness. They simply materialize, whole and themselves, in a rather stately way, and stand there, categorical in their simplicity. This can happen anywhere, not necessarily just after waking, but, characteristically, without any preparation on my part. Sometimes a single piece will appear; never more than three at once. I cannot make them all. Less than a quarter of them ever reach actuality.

Other pieces result from a more or less conscious concentration on a particular area of emotionally charged personal experience—a person, say, or a series of events, or a period in my life. I have some small degree of control over this kind of formation in that I decide whether or not to accept it. I can postpone crystallization until I have finished a previous piece that is already begun and for which I have a structure fabricated, undercoated, and ready to accept its being into itself. I try to hold the process of conception to a reasonable pace. There seems no end to this kind of formulation. These concepts hover, already complete, it would seem, on the edge of my consciousness. In the early sixties, when all this was new to me, I used to be overwhelmed and would wake up in the middle of the night flooded, inundated by peremptory demands for making these sculptures. We, they and I, have by now worked out a modus vivendi.

The force of my concentration can also be directed toward single visual events: a glimpse of radiant space, a plant in a lake, a juxtaposition of weights and shapes that matches, touches off, some powerful resonance in me. Certain sensory experiences elicit, draw forth into clarity, what visually they only infer. The laws they exemplify seem to spring from behind them, organizing a whole of form and color that lies just beyond what my senses apprehend.

Landfall, for example, came to me by itself, unexpectedly. I was driving to the studio at 1928 Calvert Street about 10:00 a.m. on a cool, rainy, windy day. I had opened the window beside me to feel the air, and rain hit my face in gusts. I put my head out into it and on the inside, behind my eyes, I was in a long, shallow, open wooden boat, multioared and with belling, rectangular, maroon sails, in wind-roughened waves. It was just after dawn; the sun, still tender, was behind me. Ahead, low on the western horizon, lay a coast just discernible as beach: landfall.

6 NOVEMBER

I was in the kitchen yesterday evening cooking dinner when my hands cutting celery were all of a sudden irradiated. I ran out into the garden and stood as if in a Bellini painting, transfixed by floods of gold. Clouds suffused with infinitely inflected shades—violets and blues and yellows—breathed against the purer blue of space, moving light itself flooded by wind. Sam leaned out his third-floor window. Mary came out on her balcony. Bear pranced around my legs. We reveled. In the afterglow, the clouds faded into grays and the clear sky deepened into the most satisfying blue, a most specific blue that is one of the reasons I live in Washington. I see it about three times a year.

7 NOVEMBER

As I came in from the studio yesterday about five o'clock, the cathedral bells burst forth with Mendelssohn's recessional wedding march. I sat down on the grass and listened and thought of the couple emerging from the austere carved portal into the brilliant afternoon light, blessed from above by tumbling bells.

The first feelings of marriage are so heavenly. I remember I used to wake up on purpose just to feel how happy I was. The heady potpourri of marriage delighted me: the lavish closeness, the just balance between delight and responsibility, household decisions, the open-endedness (the whole rest of our lives!), and the incredible beauty of being allowed to love someone as much as I wanted to.

8 NOVEMBER

I go on Monday to start teaching at the Corcoran School of Art, three morning sessions for three successive weeks as a visiting artist. I have been asked to bring slides and talk about my work, and intend to go unprepared in the dignity of my own ignorance. The roots of art could not be more mysterious to the students than to me. Art, obviously, cannot be taught. Techniques, equally obviously, can be, but these are essentially exercises. As meaningless in themselves as push-ups, they nevertheless are useful in the same way, serving to stretch and strengthen, to prepare. A concept of any importance seems to carry with it the responsibility of inventing methods for its actualization, and the energy to do so.

9 NOVEMBER

Certain concepts seem to *choose* to come into existence. For example, in 1962 I saw clearly, walked around in my mind and decided not to make, a 6' X 6' X 6' black sculpture. I can see it now perfectly plainly in the loft room of my Twining Court studio, just to the right of the entrance and illuminated from the hayloft door beyond. A few years later, I read that Tony Smith had made exactly this sculpture; and somewhat later I saw a picture of it. I have never met Tony Smith, nor has he met me. On the evidence, I can only assume that we caught the same concept.

11 NOVEMBER

My position vis-à-vis my work is becoming increasingly heuristic. The actual work seems more and more to subsume itself under an investigation the aim of which eludes my apprehension.

Until recently, this fact was obscured from me by the surge of production. This winter I cannot make new sculpture, as every penny goes into the household. There are advantages.

My health is better because I do not have to balance long hours of heavy work with other responsibilities; I actually feel buoyant some of the time. And distance from it changes my perspective on my work.

That's all very well, but I miss the flow of daily production, the pleasure of moving ahead a step or two each day toward the realization of a concept.

14 NOVEMBER

My mother began to read to me alone, as distinct from her habitual evening hour of reading aloud to her three daughters, when I was about twelve. She started with poetry—"The Forsaken Merman," "The Lady of Shalott"—and proceeded, when she saw how much I loved it, to *Jane Eyre* and *Pride and Prejudice*. We would sit near the fire in her bedroom, a tea tray on a table nearby. She read without any effort to be dramatic, but the melody of her voice and her obvious delight in introducing me to books she loved herself elicited in me an equal delight in giving her pleasure—rather a hard thing to do as she was so very self-contained—and also an impulse to write myself.

On a sheet of her blue writing paper, I wove into a medieval night a little description of the lives of lepers in the Middle Ages. The fear of leprosy was so terrible that lepers were provided with long sticks at the ends of which were attached cups that could be filled with food without the donors' risking infection. Lepers also carried bells, which they rang to warn people away from them. Never allowed to settle, nor even to pause for any length of time, they wandered in bands about Europe, living on charity. My mother read this effort of mine with affectionate respect and then, in a way that touched me very much, laid the sheet of paper carefully away in a Chinese box inlaid with mother-of-pearl flowers.

Moral choices seem more and more relative, not only to a multiplicity of possibilities but also to metaphysical scale. Not surprising, but what strikes me is an increasing awareness of calibration. I used to try to choose the lesser of two evils on this scale in a rather nearsighted way, close up. Now the choices appear more and more distinctly delineated, as if my focus had sharpened, while at the same time I seem to have moved back: I see a wider band of possible decisions. This position gives me a strength new to me, and I wonder if I am only now developing what I had always assumed I had: a conscience.

The simplistic right-wrong dichotomy never has felt true to me. I have always been aware that no one should be condemned, and have never been able to sympathize with righteous indignation except when beside myself with pain. This built-in tolerance used to feel like weakness. It took me years to get comfortable socially with what appeared to others as an insidious form of moral laziness. Abstract political action has always seemed to me almost totally meaningless, partly because of this incapacity for embracing judgments. Only individual acts feel authentic to me. It is specific moral decisions that interest me. Results seem irrelevant to these decisions, which feel to me crucial, matters of life or death.

To be morally benighted, in E. M. Forster's sense, is a fate to which I have tried to be alertly wary. If I chose to do what I felt was wrong, I tried to do so open-eyed, in the daylight of rationalization.

The change that seems to be taking place is one tending to make me equally wary of moral entrapment in my own rationalizations.

21 NOVEMBER

Paradoxically, as I begin to feel more serene, events are speeding up. Looking at my calendar, I realize that if I don't do my Christmas shopping today, I won't have time until the second week in December. And John Gossage comes this morning to go over paintings for the exhibit he is co-curating with Renato Danese at the Baltimore Museum of Art. The exhibit is primarily photography. They want one room, the same in which I exhibited sculpture in 1969, to stand apart from the photographs; the severity of my *Arundel* paintings will, they think, point up the distinctions between painting and photography. These paintings are plain enough to function like the bits of bread that wine tasters chew between sips to clear their palates.

The *Arundel* series of paintings was begun in 1973; I continue to make them from time to time, and my feeling is that I will do so for some years to come. I use only pencil and a very little white paint against a field of action I render at once active and inert by making it entirely white. In these paintings I set forth, to see for myself how they appear, what might be called the tips of my conceptual icebergs in that I put down so little of all that they refer to. I try in them to show forth the forces I feel to be a reality behind, and more interesting than, phenomena. I keep trying to catch the laws I can feel illustrated in phenomena: in meetings and just-not-meetings; in forces abutting, thrusting one against another, illuminating one another. A force is only visible in its effect, and it is the split second in which this effect becomes just barely visible that haunts me. The turns of life are secret.

These turns take place in time, and the more I think about time, the more sure I get that what my senses create is coded; that is, my experience enters my consciousness in accordance with a formula letting it into time. Ipso facto, willy-nilly, my sensory experience feels to me temporal. It has, too, a specific span and will end with my death. But that part of me that I guess I would have to call my soul not only has experience of a very different quality but also feels, clearly and unmistakably, outside of time.

25 NOVEMBER

Some part of my generation's bafflement with our offspring arises, it occurs to me, from our involvement in the Second World War. Catapulted out of our playgrounds into disaster, we were deprived of choices. A vast majority of the men and many of the women spilled into the military; those of us who remained civilians were equally caught up in the concentration of the country's effort. We had no time to experiment with our lives. We simply had to lay them on the line. And we didn't dare plan beyond the war, since we simply had to wait and see who would survive. So when we watch our children darting from flower to flower, we feel anxious, not having behind us a comparable period of youthful ranginess. There is, perhaps, a kind of jealousy too. We had to be so serious so young. And when we sorted matters out after the war, we were older, too old to play, and secretly damaged. We set about the business of living our lives as solemnly as we had tried to live in the light of our willingness to give them up.

29 NOVEMBER

An almost subliminal consciousness that privilege and its responsibilities were mine seems to have seeped into me with my mother's milk. I felt at once reenforced by it and isolated. Frightened too, as the Great Depression of the 1930s drastically cut my family's income and it became apparent to me in my late childhood that we were by no means as secure on our little island of gold as I had always taken for granted.

At that time I had a favorite dress—a delicate white voile, smocked at the neck and wrists with palest pink-and-blue embroidery. When I had outgrown it my father gathered it into other provisions he was taking to a farmer who had hurt his leg. I drove with him into the country to deliver this bounty. It was a bright frosty day and we were both rather ebullient to be on a jaunt. At that time, driving in a car was in itself something of a treat: fascinating to watch the dun land streak past us in the foreground and sedately accompany us beyond a certain distance. Naturally high-spirited himself, my father never dampened my spikes of excitement.

The farm, approached by a meandering rutted road, lay off in a flat field: random and rickety unpainted wooden structures weathered darker than the earth. Mr. Lodge had to stump quite a way to where our car was parked under a single tree beside the steep-pitched farmhouse. My father moved like quicksilver to meet him, man to man, hand to hand. I hung back, shy and suddenly made sick at heart by such bleak habitation. Near me was a stump I recognized all too well: a chicken-killing stump, mottled with dried blood. Mr. Lodge and my father stood, talking as men do in fields. They had more in common than Mr. Lodge knew. My father's income had literally been sucked into nothing by the Depression, he told me years later. My mother had to give him spending money and once threw a five-dollar bill on her bed for him to pick up—a shutter flash of what went on behind the Potemkin facades of a polite marriage. Inside our stately eighteenth-century shell, we were all scared; my mother had taken sick with fright.

I stood waiting for the men to finish talking, avoiding the stump with my eyes and feeling as cold as the earth under my feet. Finally, beckoned by Mrs. Lodge, who had opened the door and stood welcoming me, children clinging to her skirts with classic dependence, I turned. Behind her, to our mutually startled agony, loomed a classmate of mine at Easton Junior High School.

She wore the voile dress as a blouse all the rest of the year. Taller than I, her thin, roughened wrists stuck out of the transparent frills gathered by the smocking. We, who had liked each other, never met one another's eyes again. Behind my eyes she now stands clear, symbol of the betrayals sanctioned by dazingly unreal social stratification. The concept of noblesse oblige is of an impertinence unimaginable to a natural heart.

Today is Alexandra's nineteenth birthday.

When she was born, I returned to consciousness to hear the doctor say, "Give her the baby," and to feel her placed by my side. My left arm encircled her in the most natural of completions. Her eyes looked into mine, mine into hers, and I recognized her. Not only as the essence of the being who had been with me for months, but also as a person, whole, in her own right. Her solidity of character, the reliability of her understanding, her innate balance on the pivot of her self were all immediately apparent. Details followed for leisurely delight. Her texture and color echoed my husband's and mine: She had been made by us. Her rhythms matched mine. We were easy and comfortable with one another.

Mary's birth was different. I was awake when she was born. A young doctor held her up, red-faced and screaming. My whole self moved toward her. "Mary is cold," I said. "Please wrap her up." The doctor looked at me scornfully and continued to hold her as if she were a plastic doll. Tears poured out of my eyes. "She's cold," I said again, and a wave of total helplessness engulfed me as they rendered me unconscious.

Sam emerged into the world with no fuss whatsoever. He was placed near my head. Inert under a spinal anaesthetic, numb, I couldn't turn to see him over the oxygen mask. I could hear him though, and felt quite plainly that he was all right. Not serene like Alexandra, nor startled and frightened like Mary, but just naturally, matter-of-factly all right. When I laid eyes on him, hours later in my room, he looked still unborn, reluctant, steeped in some remote consciousness. A wild, windy space seemed to echo around him, and remained with him for a few months. I joined him where he was, rather than his joining me. He went about the business of growing up in the same spirit. Observing the habits of the natives, he made his way into maturity.

3 DECEMBER

On the hottest nights of my early childhood, the doors were kept open all through the house to catch a breeze. We all seem to have gone to bed at about the same time. Settling like birds on branches in the pale light, our voices dropped off one by one into the hot, sweet night.

The treasure of the South is this easy way. Some psychic armor can be dropped in the warm, undemanding atmosphere that promises safety even in the nip of winter. Squirrels who have not stretched themselves to store nuts may feel a little empty, but they will not die. The earth seems to know there is no hurry with crops. There is time for things to develop slowly. In the rocky pastures of the North even the wildflowers blossom quickly to throw their seed before the frost. I never got used to this ease, even though I lived all my childhood in the South—Maryland, Virginia, North Carolina. Out of phase, I worked and worked, ran and sweated, every minute flushed with urgency. But I always drew an obscure comfort from the slow Southern ways.

When spring came, the houses of my childhood were stripped. Rugs went into storage, baring polished floors. The furniture was covered with oatmeal linen slipcovers. Shutters were closed in the warmth of morning, opened in the cool of evening; the light was always dim, filtered greenish by the louvers. We wore cotton; even our shoes were cotton. The bedspreads were light-colored, curtains were changed to white. In some houses—not in ours, my mother's moral force never dropped—lassitude set in. The ice seemed never to stop tinkling in the lemonade pitchers.

COLUMBIA,
SOUTH CAROLINA

4 DECEMBER

As I headed south to visit and lecture at the University of South Carolina, the fields were a welcome in themselves, as were the tender light, the unassuming whitewashed clapboard houses, the leaves in lacey aureoles, the easy sweep of land like slow water. Grace dwells modestly in the Southern landscape. A tree is let alone to stand in a plowed field, though surely a vexation to cultivate around. Farm outbuildings, not in themselves anything but functional, are placed in a natural proportion.

6 DECEMBER

At one point during my lecture last night (the first lecture I have ever given), I was startled when the audience laughed spontaneously because a dog wandered into the room just as I was saying something banal about an artist "working like a dog." Not having noticed the dog, I was baffled by the laughter. But what interested me was that I felt a wave of warmth curling toward me and breaking over my head. I was given to understand that these people, invisible in the dim cavern isolated for me by the lectern's reading bulb, were *with* me. And I understood all at once why actors like to act, how power over an audience could become addictive. It began to fascinate me to try to stay a little apart from the me who was on the platform. Once or twice, I consciously let go into emotion in order to make a wind strong enough to hold and carry an idea out into the sensitive space below me.

7 DECEMBER

I did all right, I think, as a visiting artist—lecture, class visits, seminars, critiques of work—but I am left uneasy.

The balance between artist and person is somewhere in question here. It is natural for me to answer needs, to meet them and to fill them. It is not the natural woman who is the visiting artist. I feel very uncomfortable. I betray myself. Yesterday in a seminar of senior and graduate students, a student asked me why I had given up psychology for writing and writing for sculpture. I told them in a personal way. Openhearted, falling into the pit of the cult of openness, I laid myself out, dissected like a laboratory fish for them to pick over. I could so easily have said, "Because I found it didn't serve my purposes," and that statement in itself would have been enough of a lesson.

Where does the balance lie? The mother in me, the one who sees the students as if they were children wandering in a dark forest, wants to rush to them with whatever light I carry; I should stand, I now see, with that light, such as it is, and let them find me. They are not children in the first place, and not my children in the second. Insofar as I can make my own posture clear to myself, I can serve them better, leaving them more cleanly themselves and me more cleanly myself.

This is the first time I have met a situation in which a sort of myth is being put on me by a group. The students are eager for artistic salvation, the Word, given from what they conceive to be the mountaintop of the hotshot exhibited artist. I had never thought of myself defined that way, and had furthermore never realized that anyone could think that someone else could give them the Word, other than spiritually. This curious yearning for the dea ex machina has the same possibilities of egotistical fattening as the wave of warmth during the lecture: dangerous.

WASHINGTON, D.C.

9 DECEMBER

Daniel Brush, a young artist who is a friend, was able to take this trip with me and share the driving, and the last night before our return to Washington, we sat in his room and talked. He smoked one of his expensive cigars and I smoked cigarettes until we got these uneasy doubts of mine clear in our heads. I kept sitting and sitting, waiting and waiting for Daniel's intelligence to ferret out what was bothering me: a root buried deep in my muddy thinking about the artist in me. Sure enough, he finally rounded on it. "Let's say," he said, "that someone else had made your work—Beatrice Truitt, say. How would you feel about *her*?" Loyalty instantly rose in me, a wave of profound feeling about that person—I could see her—who worked day after day into dark winter evenings in her quilted athletic suit, booted and hatted against the cold, putting on "just one more coat" before piling the painty brushes into the children's old Easter basket to take home for washing. In that second, it became clear to me: I was responsible for her, to Beatrice, to Anne Truitt, who had worked and worked, whose work, against all likelihood, had been recognized to be art of some quality. It was Anne Truitt who had been invited to lecture, to speak to students about their work, to share her experience. I, Anne, have other experience, private experience, as useful perhaps, but to be shared by choice in other contexts, never again to be confused with Anne Truitt's experience in art.

I cannot say how relieved I felt when I finally returned to my own room to cherish my lightheartedness into sleep. Anne Truitt and I are together now, free of one another, at one another's service.

On our way home Daniel and I circled through Asheville, North Carolina, where I lived from the age of fourteen until my departure for Boston in 1943.

My parents' graves are marked by two rectangular granite stones laid level with the sloping ground. As I looked down on them, I slipped in the snow, fell almost on top of them, and felt in that second the sharp loss of their comfort. Rooted at last, one from St. Louis, one from Boston, they dimly echo an American restlessness. Pioneers to what end? They never really belonged to the Eastern Shore of Maryland, and indeed, as far as I know, they only settled there because my father's sister had married a man who lived on the peninsula. Their lives had no objective purpose, were unconnected to any real aim other than the dignified and honorable spending of day into night. I cannot, in my own person engaged hot and heavy with life, really understand how they lived.

My mother survived for four months after she was operated on for a brain tumor. We took care of her at home, with two nurses around the clock. This was a bittersweet time, every moment counted. I read her *Howards End*, a book we had both enjoyed reading together before. We were cozy. I sang her favorite hymns to lull her to sleep, as she had so often sung them to me in other twilights. We worked on certain exercises that would supposedly strengthen the muscles of her left arm, useless after the operation. The exercises I knew to be useless too, but knew with equal certainty that effort, the habit of a lifetime, would make her comfortable with herself.

During her last hours, the doctor suggested that she take sips of wine. Just before she lost consciousness, my mother, with great sweetness, looked up at me and asked gently, "Do they want me to take this to the very end, Annie, dear?" I said, "Yes." She nodded a dignified obedience. Selfless, with a faith so simple as to require no articulation, she was restless only about my father and my sisters. Reassured, she slipped into a coma and I heard her breath stop, leaving a filled silence.

My father died in a hospital, just short of his eightieth birthday, with something of the same matter-of-factness. During the hours of his last night, he roused once to ask the time, and then sank tranquilly into an unconsciousness that trailed into death.

Now they lie side by side on an alien hill.

Perhaps it is I who am an alien there. I never settled in Asheville, for by the time we moved there I was well on my way into my own life, fully conscious that my way led me out. And I was glad that it did—not in rejection, but in pleasure that my adult strength was coming in to me. I have seen the same realization dawn on my two daughters and have rejoiced with them in memory of my own lift into freedom.

14 DECEMBER

Yesterday was a thoroughly human day. Alexandra and I shopped together and ate lunch in the car, munching on delicious delicatessen cheese sandwiches with swaths of butter and mustard. In the evening Sam and a friend of his and I talked in the kitchen while I cooked, the boys sprawled over the little blue chairs, all of us indulging in the pleasure of chat.

18 DECEMBER

Once I sailed in Nova Scotia with a man who put his ship so close into the wind that I stood thigh deep in the ocean, flattened against the deck behind me as I held on to the lines, body thrust almost perpendicular into the cold, curling waves.

The New York art world is like that. The artist is put into an acute balance of risk. Other situations in my professional experience scarcely resemble this total challenge. I have been showing in New York since 1963, three one-artist shows at the André Emmerich Gallery, with another due this spring, and one retrospective exhibit at the Whitney Museum last winter. Certainly I have cut my teeth.

Artists are thrust straight up against the wave of their ambition in the world as well as their ambition for their work. Unless they like being rolled over and over on the sharp pebbles of their own inconsistencies, they have to dive through this wave into understanding. There is a cant going around now that this is more difficult for women. I don't feel comfortable generalizing about it, engaging as it does idiosyncratic solutions to the vexing problem of the individual's adjustment to being an artist in public view. I do know that at my back I always feel the cave of womanhood. I can retreat into it and lick my wounds, cooking and tending my children and, when I was married, sheltering under my husband. And I also know that I have to guard against allowing myself to be defined, either by myself or by others, in traditional, sociological terms. The nub of my discomfort is a feeling more or less conscious that it is unbecoming for a woman to feel broad-scoped ambition at all, much less to try to achieve it.

Webster defines ambition as "an eager or inordinate desire for preferment, honor, superiority, power, or attainment." He extrapolates that "ambition has personal advancement or preferment as its end," and adds rather sweetly, "It may be praiseworthy." He gives as its synonym aspiration, defined as "a longing for what is elevated or above one." Aspiration derives from the Latin verb *aspirare* from *ad* plus *spirare*, to breathe, a derivation that places it in the category of the most natural act of our lives.

Tradition has never denied aspiration to women. Indeed, they have been held in honor, not only as objects to which men aspire but also as vessels of high principles, high hopes, "A good wife" stamps a seal of approval on a man. The two-gunned, two-fisted western hero always has a delicate lady with whom he shares a sunset after he has finished shooting. It is ambition, the desire to experience for themselves the worldly results of their own achieved aspirations, that women have culturally been called down for. This is truly unfair. Born human, they have logically as natural a right to ambition as men. Denied it, they are denied the possibilities of the growth that ambition demands for its successful achievement.

The cave of womanhood feels cozy to me, and I shall always, I think, retreat to it with the comfortable feeling that I am where I should be in some sense deeper than words can articulate. So men may feel about some cave of manhood that I can only imagine. There is sturdy common sense in accepting the differences between men and women as salt. But because womanhood is "home" to me does not mean that I wish to stay home all the time. The cave would become fetid if I never went out. I have too much energy, too much curiosity, too much force to remain so confined. Whole areas of myself would either atrophy or sour. If I wish to be responsible to myself, and I do, I have to pursue my aspirations. In the course of doing so, I find myself confronted by the necessity to recognize my own ambition. If I wish to make the highest art I can, I have—to pick my words from Webster—"an eager desire for superiority or attainment."

I do not, however, think it "inordinate." Gerard Manley Hopkins points out that just as "to every moral act, being right or wrong, there belongs, of the nature of things, reward or punishment, so to every form perceived by the mind belongs, in the nature of things, admiration or the reverse." (*Poems and Prose of Gerard Manley Hopkins*, W. H. Gardner, ed., New York: Penguin Books, 1953, p. 183.) In this context, one which more or less fits my own observations, my ambition to see my work meet whatever it, in its own nature, calls forth in response is logical. I need not feel ashamed and can identify such feeling as a cultural vestige to which I could only cling for neurotic reasons.

Have I been, I ask myself, in my lifelong efforts to achieve some modicum of my aspirations, ambitious beyond this meet response? Aside from some raring part of myself who always wants to be, as my father used to say, "the bride at the wedding and the corpse at the funeral," I think I can honestly say that I have not. I like to win, but, if I am to be content, I have to feel that I have won without paying a price that would outrage my principles. These principles preclude my doing what would be in my own eyes venal. They set guidelines to which I try to be alert, not from any particular virtue, but to spare myself remorse.

So I end up in the position of a reasonably aspiring, reasonably ambitious man, no more and no less boundaried by my own character. This is lucky, because I cannot help doing the work I do, which feels to me as vital as my breath. I should not like to be in a position in which I could not breathe for fear of going against what I feel is right. But, were I a man, I would not have had laboriously to pick my way through such an obvious train of thought to such an obvious conclusion.

23 DECEMBER

Apparently there is green paint on the back of my hair. An acquaintance remarked on it, calling it "chartreuse"—to my eye a horrid color and not at all the glowing green, so multiple in its inflections, with which I have thought myself painting *17th Summer*. Once again I am brought face-to-face with the fact that I cannot gauge, except within a rough range, what other people see. For him, *17th Summer* would appear to be chartreuse, purple, and blue—of heaven knows what specificity. It takes a certain stubbornness to keep on making objects within the strict discipline of my senses. There is a taproot of selfishness. In narrow fact, I am making them only for my own perception.

24 DECEMBER

I feel a little pulled at the seams. Too much is happening too fast for me to integrate. Life unrolls like a Mack Sennett comedy. The film is so speeded up that events threaten to splinter into nonsense.

1975

1 JANUARY

The ground smells of spring. I am glad to be delivered once more from the dark solstice into the turn toward growth. January is my favorite month, when the light is plainest, least colored. And I like the feeling of beginnings.

3 JANUARY

In 1933, when I was twelve, the axe fell on the sunny progression of my days. The Depression, which temporarily annihilated my father's income and cut my mother's, laid waste to my childhood suddenly and unexpectedly. It seemed to me that one day all was as it had always been and the next both my parents were sick; our old nurse, retired; our cook, who had also been with us for years, replaced; and I was left virtually in charge of the household. My mother was in a hospital in Baltimore for almost the entire winter of 1933–34. My father, stricken beyond his capacity to rise above his circumstances, took to getting "sick." He had "flu" regularly, and gradually I understood that this meant he got drunk regularly. I was profoundly ashamed of him. Considering it now, I wonder why some grown-up person didn't take charge more. My parents had friends. But no one did anything, and I was left to gather my forces and give what orders were given to run the house and to see that the schedule was maintained, cheerlessly but competently. I did my homework in my usual place, at a small, delicate French desk in the library, but nothing else was as it had been.

Now that alcoholism is recognized as a commonplace and shameless disorder, it is difficult to realize that even so short a time ago as my own childhood there was no help offered in such situations. The doctor who came to see my father when matters became critical, and who ordered him a nurse for a while, was kind enough; but I picked up his embarrassment. In response, I closed my doors and retired, as I had observed my mother doing, into routine and pride.

And so the whole world in which I had bloomed so happily, enjoying my crises as well as my pleasures, was overtaken by a twilight. But that, too, ended when, in the spring of 1934, my sisters and I went to spend the summer with my mother's sister, my dear aunt Nancy, on her farm in Virginia. The summer stretched into the winter, my parents continued to be sick, the house in Easton was sold, and in the fall of 1935 our whole family moved south to Asheville, North Carolina. But by that time I had changed. Nurtured among seven children, we three and my four cousins, I had recovered my childishness and then begun to outgrow it more naturally.

3 JANUARY

The exhibit of the *Arundel* paintings at the Baltimore Museum of Art is now beginning to magnetize events. The paintings pull together in my head. An exhibit exists long before it is installed, and is delivered by a series of familiar decisions and actions.

4 JANUARY

The Renaissance emphasis on the individuality of the artist has been so compounded by the contemporary fascination with personalities that artists stand in danger of plucking the feathers of their own breast, licking up the drops of blood as they do so, and preening themselves on their courage. It is not surprising that some come to suicide, the final screw on this spiral of self-exploitation. And particularly sad because the artist's impulse is inherently generous. But what artists have to give and want to give is rarely matched and met. The public, themselves deprived of the feeling of community that grants due proportion to everyone's self-expression, yearn over the artist in some special way because he or she seems to have the magic to wrench color and meaning from their bleached lives. The artist gives them themselves. They can even buy themselves.

6 JANUARY

While we were visiting in England during the summer of my eleventh year, my mother took me alone one afternoon to Westminster Abbey. We entered through the great portal and walked down the nave, stopping off here and there to see the tombs of people who had been—until the moment I saw the places where they were buried—abstractions, storybook people. We then made our way out into the cloisters, and there my mother explained to me the construction of the cathedral. As she spoke, I saw with utter clarity how the outside of the building matched the inside, and felt with a lifting of my heart the immense interior space upheld by the buttresses and flying buttresses that proliferated one against the other to raise the walls and to anchor them to the supporting earth. In a few brief words, she gave me the concept of intelligent and ingenious construction, of solution; I saw clearly that people had had an idea and then had thought up a way to make that idea real. And also that the idea had to do with their feelings about the nature of God, their highest feelings, those about which they felt most passionate. I saw too that it must have been an exceedingly difficult feat, and that many people had had to work together on a common plan. The lives of those who conceived the abbey, and those who had worked on it, and those who were buried in it came together in my mind. Theirs was a fellowship both anonymous and famous, dedicated to the realization of their highest ideals.

All this reverberated within me, but what most struck me was the actual construction itself, the solution of the apparently insoluble problem of raising walls so high into the air. From then on, I looked at buildings with a different, more speculative eye. How did they fit? How did the outside match the inside? And, by the extrapolation of this curiosity as I grew older, I became sensitive to how every appearance has something inside that explains how it looks.

Reverence, nurtured by our evening prayers, which my mother always heard at our bedsides, and by the Sunday school to which we went regularly in Christ Church next door to our house, had long been one of the deepest roots of my feeling. It had not yet occurred to me that this feeling could be expressed. Westminster Abbey taught me that, given intelligence, industry, and passion, such awe could be made actually to exist, transmuted into symbol.

7 JANUARY

Of all the Ten Commandments, "Thou shalt not murder" always seemed to me the one I would have to worry least about, until I got old enough to see that there are many different kinds of death, not all of them physical. There are murders as subtle as a turned eye. Dante was inspired to install Satan in ice, cold indifference being so common a form of evil.

10 JANUARY

There is an appalling amount of mechanical work in the artist's life: lists of works with dimensions, prices, owners, provenances; lists of exhibitions with dates and places; bibliographical material; lists of supplies bought, storage facilities used. Records pile on records. This tedious, detailed work, which steadily increases if the artist exhibits to any extent, had been something of a surprise to me. It is all very well to be entranced by working in the studio, but that has to be backed up by the common sense and industry required to run a small business. In trying to gauge the capacity of young artists to achieve their ambition, I always look to see whether they seem to have this ability to organize their lives into an order that will not only set their hands free in the studio but also meet the demands their work will make upon them when it leaves the studio. The "enemies of promise," in Cyril Connolly's phrase, are subtle, guileful, and resourceful. Talent is mysterious, but the qualities that guard, foster, and direct it are not unlike those of a good quartermaster.

II JANUARY

An exhibit that is coming along well is cheerful. Yesterday John Gossage and Renato Danese, the co-curators of the Baltimore Museum of Art exhibit, and I strode around the museum as if on our native heath, making decisions together, with the zest of experience. This lightheartedness in no way denies our knowledge that much could go wrong before our concept of the exhibit becomes real.

The point at which decision is brought to bear on process is that at which two opposing forces meet and rebound, leaving an interval in which a third force can act. The trick of acting is to catch this moment. When it all happens well, a happy feeling of swinging from event to event results, a sort of gymnastic pleasure. Yesterday Renato thought an exhibition room should be unified by pigeon gray; John thought the photographs would line up into nonentity in such a flat environment. They turned to me. I suggested a third solution incorporating both insights; we all rose to it and took the wave of decision as one.

It was Gurdjieff who dissected this process for me to examine, and I like to watch it happening. His analysis of process into octaves is also fascinating to me, and very helpful. An undertaking, he says, begins with a surge of energy that carries it a certain distance toward completion. There then occurs a drop in energy, which must be lifted back to an effective level by conscious effort, in my experience by bringing to bear hard purpose. It is here that years of steady application to a specific process can come into play. It is, however, in the final stage, just before completion, that Gurdjieff says pressure mounts almost unendurably to a point at which it is necessary to bring to bear an even more special kind of effort. It is at this point, when idea is on the verge of bursting into physicality, that I find myself meeting maximum difficulty. I sometimes have the curious impression that the physical system seems in its very nature to *resist* its invasion by idea. The desert wishes to lie in the curves of its own being: It resists the imposition of the straight line across its natural pattern. Matter itself seems to have some mysterious intransigency.

It is at this critical point that most failures seem to me to occur. The energy required to push the original concept into actualization, to finish it, has quite a different qualitative feel from the effort needed to bring it to this point. It is this strange, higher-keyed energy to which I find I have to pay attention—to court, so to speak, by living in a particular way. Years of training build experience capable of holding a process through the second stage. The opposition of purpose to natural indolence, the friction of this opposition, maintained year after year, seems to create a situation that attracts this mysterious third force, the curious fiery energy required to raise an idea into realization. Whether or not it does so attract remains a mystery.

The Baltimore exhibit is in the second stage of this process. We are bringing our experience to it and are prepared to bear down hard through the final stage. Whether the exhibit will lift into the light in which we conceive it to exist remains in jeopardy.

The east-west-north-south coordinates, latitude and longitude, of my sculptures exactly reflect my concern with my position in space, my location. This concern, an obsession since earliest childhood, must have been the root of my 1961 decision—taken unconsciously in a wave of conviction so total as to have been unchallenged by logic—to place my sculptures on their own feet as I am on mine. This is a straight, clear line between my life and my work.

14 JANUARY

Yesterday morning I wrote the lecture I am to give at the Baltimore Museum of Art. The shape of my work's development becomes a little clearer every time I am forced to articulate it. I noticed for the first time yesterday, in reviewing my slides, how rapidly the scale of the earliest work in 1961–62 changed from that of fence to that of human beings, and then to that which comprehended human beings as incidental within its own range.

The *Arundel* paintings were picked up yesterday afternoon, departing into a twilight dancing with large fluffy snow flakes as white as themselves. No amount of experience seems to dull the prick of separation. Quick, not entertained, but inevitable. Now the paintings are covered with the same quiet attention with which I follow my children in my mind.

A day of rest idles my mind into a nullity out of which I am refreshed. Lying under my warm covers, I spent most of yesterday wandering over the Near East with Alexander the Great, conquering my way to the river Hyphasis and turning back toward Macedonia as reluctantly as he did. There is always that wrench, not being able to do it all.

Military tactics interest me very much. Wellington's choice of ground at Waterloo, his disposition of his forces, his timing, and above all his resolute decision to stand and die or stand and live, brace my heart for lesser battles. Alexander was an inspired tactician. At Jhelum his horses, maddened with fear, refused to advance across a river into King Paros's elephants, the front line of an army superbly trained and many times the size of Alexander's. Calmly setting up a pattern of behavior calculated to lead an intelligent observer to conclude that he intended to stand siege on his side of the river until the seasonal waters fell, Alexander seized a night of storm, crossed the river under its thunder and lightning, and stampeded the elephants with rattling Scythian chariots and flights of arrows. Thus freed to use his nimble cavalry, he moved in authoritatively to decimate his enemy. He just plain outthought King Paros. Obviously, he could not have known that he was going to be successful. He simply made as intelligent a plan as he could and then acted on it with all the force at his command. It is said that he always slept well on the eve of battle. His cardinal tactical principle he derived from Epaminondas: "The quickest and most economical way of winning a military decision is to defeat the enemy not at his weakest but at his strongest point." (Peter Green, *Alexander the Great*, New York: Praeger, 1970.) Just so have I found that a direct confrontation of difficulties at their worst is the best starting point for action.

17 JANUARY

The *Arundel* paintings are installed in the Baltimore Museum of Art. An easy installation. We reduced their number to eight and they seemed to place themselves, even to stretch themselves luxuriously once they were hung. I wish I could be as serene as they looked yesterday after we had finished. I can, and I think I do, use my head on the business of exhibiting, but there is an irreducible strain. It is easier than last winter but—I guess because I am trying to do it all more plainly, without excitement—my spirit rises only sluggishly to the challenge.

19 JANUARY

But there are pleasures too in exhibiting. Flowers abound all over the house; friends encircle me. This is the period I always think of as comparable to the protection given an elephant in labor. When, after almost two years of gestation, she is ready to deliver her child, the herd forms a circle around her. A particular friend helps her in her labor and coaxes the baby into vitality. The circle remains intact until the mother and child are ready to travel. Then the herd moves on, larger by one member.

The Baltimore exhibit is now open. The reaction was exactly what it always is. Some, most, simply cannot "see" the work at all. One of my children overheard the scornful remark, "Well, I never did think Anne Truitt was much of an artist."

This failure to see is not only psychological but also can apparently be physical. A physicist explained to me during dinner at the museum last night about the macula lutea, a yellow retinal filter that circumscribes the fovea. Foveal vision, which determines our apprehension of line, is limited by its cellular nature to the perception of red and green only. This perceptive acuity apparently varies little from person to person. The saturation of yellow in the macula lutea, however, varies considerably. It is the nature of this filter that determines our perception of blues. Thus, some people, those with concentrated yellow in the macula lutea, are literally unable to see close changes of hue on the blue end of the spectrum.

I always take off my glasses to mix color. This must be an instinctive shift in attention away from foveal vision, specific and limited to red-green sensitivity, toward a concentration on the entire possible range of subtle hue and value discrimination. In addition, since all glass absorbs blue light, removing my glasses increases the amount of blue light reaching my eyes.

These facts seem to me relevant to the apprehension of the *Arundel* paintings, which depend for their perception on both foveal and nonfoveal vision. The lines in them are sometimes so widely spaced that they cannot be seen simultaneously, and the fields of white in which these lines act depend for their understanding on peripheral vision; that is, on the entire range of sight from all the way left to all the way right.

Earlier this morning I was swept by waves of sorrow as imperative as the blizzard now blowing outside my window. A memento mori. The *Arundel* paintings—which came in, so to speak, from nowhere—will remain here "in the where" while I will ultimately go out into nowhere. I rejoice in their existence. But each objectification is a subjective diminishment.

23 JANUARY

Are there wounds that never heal? Yes. When accurately pricked, they bleed as freshly, but not as long, as when first pierced.

I like sometimes to think of my past as laid out like the relief maps of my childhood: Particolored, motley-textured, lush here, arid there, pocked with craters events have blown or scraped out. Certain areas are bogged with pain, but there are tufts of tough grass that I have nurtured carefully so I can traverse these places with relative safety. Occasionally my foot slips, and I plunge.

24 JANUARY

Reaction to the *Arundel* exhibit seems to be rather more than negative, verging on the vicious.

A mystery confounds the problem of industry in art. In the last analysis, to work is simply not enough. But we have to act as if it were, leaving reward aside.

People who set their sails into art tend to work very hard. They train themselves in school; they practice and they read and they think and they talk. But for most of them there seems to be a more or less conscious cutoff point. It can be a point in time: "I will work until I am twenty-one [twenty-five, thirty, or forty]." Or a point in effort: "I will work three hours a day [or eight, or ten]." Or a point in pleasure: "I will work unless . . ." and here the "enemies of promise" harry the result. These are personal decisions, more or less of individual will. They depend on the scale of values according to which artists organize their lives. Artists have a modicum of control. Their development is open-ended. As the pressure of their work demands more and more of them, they can stretch to meet it. They can be open to themselves, and as brave as they can be to see who they are, what their work is teaching them. This is never easy. Every step forward is a new clearing through a thicket of reluctance and habit and natural indolence. And all the while they are at the mercy of events. They may have a crippling accident, or may find themselves yanked into a lifelong responsibility such as the necessity to support themselves and their families. Or a war may wipe out the cultural context on which they depend. Even the most fortunate have to adjust the demands of a personal obsession to the demands of daily life.

I have found this adjustment tricky. I began working in sculpture in 1948. Married, I had to fit my own work into a schedule of shopping, cooking, housecleaning, entertaining, and—very often—moving from city to city. My first child was born in 1955, followed by two more in 1958 and 1960. By 1961, when all of a sudden my work took a quantum jump into a range I recognized as preemptive, demanding, undeniable, totally categorical for me, I had a large and complicated setup within which I had to operate.

My husband was an enterprising journalist, which in Washington means a lot of entertaining and being entertained—very time-consuming, and energy-consuming too. I was expected to enter into his life with commitment to his career. And, within the context of marriage as we had defined it without thinking too much about it, I felt I should do so. My husband and I were both hospitable. We had houseguests continuously. Having been traditionally brought up, it did not occur to me to fight against this situation. I simply took it for granted that I had to fit what I wanted to do within it. My children were at that time six, three, and one. Their care came first. Doctors' appointments, reading to them, rocking the baby to sleep, car pools—all that had to be done, and done as well as I could, before I could turn to myself. Confronted by this situation, I made two major decisions.

The first was to invest in myself, as needed, the money I had inherited from my family. I simply poured my capital into my work. Fortunately—and indeed, more than fortunately, crucially—my husband underwrote the household expenses and I was able to have a very faithful live-in maid who was my friend as well and who shared household responsibilities with me. So I used my financial resources to the hilt.

The second major decision was to increase my energy output and to use it as wisely and as fully as I could. Again fortunately, during the years from 1948 to 1961 I had formed the habit of working in my studio almost every single day. Rain or shine, eager or dragging my feet, I just plain forced myself to work. This habitual discipline came up under me to support my revved-up schedule. I simply got up early every morning and worked straight through the day in one way or another, either in my household or in my studio. Before I went to sleep, I loosely organized the following day's schedule—loosely because there were, of course, always unexpected events. But I tried to hold course in accordance with my values: first—husband, children, household; second—my work. The periods of time left over from my practical responsibilities were spent in the studio. If there were fifteen minutes between shopping and carpool, I used them. If I had an hour, or two hours, I rejoiced, but didn't even waste time feeling happy, just worked.

Something graceful and to be cherished, something delicate and sweet fell by the board with this obsession, which, in essence, still remains a mystery to me. Why am I so obsessed? I do not know.

One element is clear, however, and that is that the capacity to work feeds on itself and has its own course of development. This is what artists have going for them. From 1948 to 1961, I worked out of obsession, but obsession served by guilt: I felt uncomfortable if I failed to work every possible working day. In 1961, to my total astonishment, the guilt dropped away, replaced by an effortless, unstrained, well-motivated competence that I very soon was able simply to take for granted.

25 JANUARY

Two floors underground in the Washington Hilton Hotel yesterday afternoon, elevated by six inches of platform skirted with a red-pleated frill, I sat on a panel of five artists discussing how to endure in art. We said a good deal, but it all came down in the end to a stubborn feeling on our part that you just had to keep on going no matter what, and in the face of not knowing what the results would be. It was Jack Tworkov who said it best. "Sometimes when you finish a painting," he said, "you look at it and it looks all right and that's a little touch of grace."

Alexander Giampietro, who taught me sculpture at the Institute of Contemporary Art in Washington from September 1948 to December 1949, appeared at the discussion. He is a noble man. I am blessed to have had him as a teacher and always knew so, but know it better in my maturity.

Alex's Italianness had a lot to do with placing my feet firmly in art. He radiates the Renaissance. His natural setting is Florence, in some open wooden structure strewn with tools and blocks of marble, ringing with the blows of mallet on chisel, and flooded with honey yellow light moted with marble dust. When I studied with him, I saw him thus, he the master, I the apprentice. I copied from him the muscular patterns of art, in a glow of enthusiasm partly generated by Alex's vitality and partly by my own romantic imagination and partly by a natural aptitude for movement, for action. And, as cogently, by my own passionate interest in process. I learned with the intentness of the child who had stood on short legs to watch the moist bricks go into the kiln and come out a different color, hot and hard.

Giampietro's training was as natural to me as breathing. I never stopped to question or even to think much. I just absorbed every single bit of information with every single bit of my body. The warmth of hardening plaster deepened my love for its having lent itself fluently to my hand. Plaster has such grace. Working with it is like making love. And the same with clay. The fascination of mixing clay: the wedging of earth colors, minerals, back into the earth in order to make a new earth all of your own conception, consciously brought into being. The delicate strength of tools for work in clay and plaster; the ways in which they adroitly extend the sensual ability of the hand; their actual beauty in themselves—wire bound to wood, steel-toothed and curved and pimpled with rasp. My hands loved, too, the feel between them of what they had formed. This love is like that I later felt for my babies, the same quality of profound sensuous satisfaction. Nothing is missing from it. All is there, globed, whole, full, perfect.

It was not my eyes or my mind that learned. It was my body. I fell in love with the process of art, and I've never fallen out of it. I even loved the discomforts. At first my arms ached and trembled for an hour or so after carving stone; I remember sitting on the bus on the way home and feeling them shake uncontrollably. My blouse size increased by one as my shoulders broadened with muscle. My whole center of gravity changed. I learned to move from a center of strength and balance just below my navel. From this place, I could lift stones and I could touch the surface of clay as lightly as a butterfly's wing. I watched Alex move, and I copied. I watched how he paced himself, never hurrying and never stopping—except to sit in the sun occasionally—and I copied. I listened when he spoke of the turns of the earth and the moon and the stars in an order of which we, in our bustling studio, were a part. We must never forget this order, he kept saying, always place ourselves in proportion to it, always resound with it. I felt as if I had come home as I listened. When his seventh child was due to be born, he waited for the birth on the turn of the moon. On the twilight November evenings just before Sam's birth, I remember looking at the sky and waiting myself for the moon's turn, which, sure enough, heralded his birth as it had that of Alex's child.

Never in all those golden quattrocento months during which I sat at Alex's feet was there a tawdry syllable. His purity enclosed and guarded ours. The world was, of course, out there. Occasionally I would pick up from him some anxiety, or we students would mention personal troubles, but only in intervals of application to our study. Talk about exhibiting was very rare. We were encouraged to feel secure, like the children we were, in art. Alex guarded our artistic childhood so we could mature like melons in the sun, growing slowly into sweetness. When I left his workshop, I took with me as his legacy this feeling of security, and it remains with me. In my studio I feel at home with myself, peaceful at heart, remote from the world, totally immersed in a process so absorbing as to be its own reward.

And so I was saved, in great part by the sanity of Giampietro's purity of heart and purpose, from the suffering the panel discussion of the 24th laid bare to my view: that of thinking of worldly result in the studio.

3 FEBRUARY

Yesterday I stood at the lectern in the Baltimore Museum of Art with my feet flat on the floor, my back straight, and my arms stretched comfortably out to the sides of the shelf. Twice my shoulders felt stiff and I relaxed them. Once I heard my voice tremble and I strengthened it. Speaking at first into a dark pit that only later as my eyes adjusted to the light became visible as an audience, I felt alone, as I do in the studio. This is a good feeling for me. I was able to speak straight out of it.

Only one saddening note. My oldest friend, whom I have known ever since I can remember any friend at all, had driven some miles to hear me talk. When I saw her standing patiently at the back of a group waiting to speak to me after the lecture, I felt the bleak edge of separation, one of the subtle prices implicit in being a public figure, even in so modest a way.

Last night I slept well, and awoke this morning refreshed. I have quite a new feeling that I will be able to do this kind of lecture again with relative competence and ease. The experience gained at the Corcoran School of Art and at the University of South Carolina, plus the fact that I had thoroughly prepared and rehearsed the lecture, have combined to place me on a firm foundation.

During the question-and-answer period, I was asked where I thought art came from, from what part of the mind. I answered that I did not know but I thought it possible to put one's self in the way of art much in the same way that cloistered devotees place themselves in the way of religious experience. Art comes, if we are blessed with what Jack Tworkov called a "little touch of grace," into the highest part of the mind, that with which we can know the presence of God. But we have to pay attention to that area in order to notice the grace, or even perhaps to attract it.

When I painted a chair recently, I noticed that I put the paint on indifferently, smoothly but without particular attention. The results were satisfactory but not in any sense beautiful. Does the attention in itself with which paint is applied in art actually change the effect of the paint? Does the kind of consciousness with which we act determine the quality of our actions? It would follow, if this were true, that the higher the degree of consciousness, the higher the quality of the art. I think it likely. Training in art is, then, a demand that students increase the consciousness with which they employ techniques that are, in themselves, ordinary.

7 FEBRUARY

Intellect can examine the force commonly called "God" only when it is manifest in phenomena, themselves limited to sensory apprehension. Its very use logically precludes knowledge of the force itself, such use being ipso facto rooted in duality: subject and object. This sound argument leads me flat up against the realization that, as clearly as I have ever known any fact, I know the existence of God. What with, is the question. It must necessarily be with equipment sensitive to a different range from that of my ordinary senses, which are firmly organized by my intellect. Here the facts of my own experience lead me, inexorably, to the postulation of a range in my own sensitivity that lies beyond my immediate consciousness.

9 FEBRUARY

I feel a little brittle and have decided to try to go to Ossabaw Island, off the coast of Georgia, for two weeks in late March. Work thins me out. We, my sculptures and I, are symbiotic while they are in process. My energy nourishes them to completion. And their completion depletes me.

Last night I didn't take off my work clothes until bedtime,

hoping to get back into the studio, but was in the end too tired to go. It just doesn't work well for me to push like that. And dinner is no fun for the children and me if I am on the wing.

Ramon Osuna of Pyramid Gallery here in Washington has suggested that I have an exhibit in the spring. And André Emmerich and I have decided to postpone my exhibit in New York with him until April 12th. For some mysterious reason, maybe because this particular exhibit for his gallery keeps kaleidoscoping in my mind, I feel enormously relieved, let off the hook. He proposes a small sculpture exhibit in the little room in which he customarily shows drawings at the Fifty-seventh Street gallery. So the plans fall into place: the Emmerich exhibit will open on April 12th and the Pyramid, also a sculpture exhibit, three days later.

I am glad that both will be in the spring. There is a grievous feeling around these days and we pick it up through our psychological pores, like pickles in brine. I understand the blessing of laughter better than I used to, having—I hope—outlasted some of the portentous solemnity to which, when I am tired or frightened or insecure, I am sadly prone. A light heart has more virtue than romantic agony.

At the beach a few days ago, sitting in my long wrapper and my Pooh Bear jacket on a round piling stump, steaming coffee mug in hand, facing across the pale sand into the rising sun, I thought of what to do with the sunrise. (Why, I incidentally ask myself, do I always feel compelled to turn everything into something else? A tiresome habit of my mind, I sometimes think.)

If I used paint, I should theoretically be able to convey the visual facts clearly, except, obviously, to those who are blind. But here, assuming a realistic picture is proposed, the difficulties are daunting. Change is easy to convey in writing. In painting, a choice of moment must be made. The delicate changes implicit in rising are so the essence of sunrise that this choice automatically enforces an almost fatal limitation. Naturalistic paintings of nature generally tend toward this kind of dry declamation. In order to convey the essence of a whole range of visual experience in time, I would thus be forced out of naturalistic representation and into a language of art as complicated as words—and more irritating to people. No one questions the fact that verbal language has to be learned, but the commonplaceness of visual experience betrays art; people tend to assume that, because they can see, they can see art. So in the end my ability to convey my experience of the sunrise would depend, first, on my having mastered an abstract language and, second, on someone else's having mastered it too.

19 FEBRUARY

February derives from *februare*: to purify, to cleanse. Air, trees, bushes, grass, earth, jonquil shoots, forsythia buds—and us. Fresh January is quickening into the thrumming of spring.

On my fifty-fourth birthday I will go to Ossabaw Island, now, like Yaddo, a place generously offered to those who need quiet and time to work.

In 1949, the Institute of Contemporary Art mounted a school exhibit. We students, bearing our work, trooped down to a huge shed on K Street housing the city food market to which farmers brought their produce for sale. There, among the chickens hanging by their yellow legs and the piles of freshly baked bread and the tomatoes, rhubarb, green peppers, and potatoes, amidst the cries of vendors and the push of housewives, we set forth our wares. That, my first experience in exhibiting, was not unlike every other experience of exhibiting since.

At such an opening last night I encountered the director of the Baltimore Museum of Art. He told me that there has been something of a clamor in Baltimore to the effect that the public's money is being misspent placing on display in the city museum such meaningless works as the *Arundel* paintings. So vitriolic were these comments that the mayor of Baltimore telephoned to assure him that he stood behind the museum's decisions.

I understand with my mind that outrage can be a kind of confirmation of the work's validity. Obviously, it is stating *something* if it evokes so strong a reaction. But I am left a little more lonely. Not much, but a definite little.

Last night four women sat at my dining-room table in the candlelight: one in her forties; one in her thirties; Mary, sixteen; and I, fifty-three. We walked warily and rather sadly around the fact that no one was going to look after us but ourselves. The idea of being protected by men dies hard. We had all (except perhaps Mary) given up the feeling that such protection is our *right*. But we all, in varying degrees, decreasing with age, cherished some small hope of the idyllic warmth of male shelter.

I have come, even so recently as within the last month, to the verge of preferring to look after myself. This is partly because it begins to seem financially possible. *Arundel* XIV sold yesterday. *Summer Sentinel* is out on approval. The University of Maryland has invited me to lecture. I have been paid by the Baltimore Museum of Art and by the University of South Carolina.

The crux of the matter seems to me to be the true danger of emotional dependence. Obviously, there are situations in which physical dependence is a virtual necessity; in sickness or disability, in temporary conditions like childbirth. When you love someone, there is a joy in meeting these situations with instinctive generosity, total support, and also in accepting the bounty of someone with whom you are in a bond of love. The danger lies in the cultivation of mutual dependence, the "I need you, you need me" definition of a relationship in a continuing, habitual stance. If I believe that someone needs me, I recognize a weakness in that person, and vice versa. To meet such a need without trying to formulate some understanding of it nourishes the weakness. Shortly, a folie à deux is established and preconception begins to define the territory of one another's development. The two people can, and almost always do, slip into the sad dilemma of not liking the roles they have set up for one another. This is, I think, the root of many marital failures. The only viable relationship between a man and a woman seems to me to be a relationship of peers.

24 FEBRUARY

I now have eight pieces of sculpture going simultaneously. This is more than I am accustomed to handling at one time, and I feel the strain. I leave for Ossabaw Island three weeks from yesterday. By that time, these pieces must be finished.

25 FEBRUARY

The kitchen sink is stopped up. At 11:30 last night, after the guests had left and the children were in bed, I was dipping greasy water from it into the downstairs lavatory, back and forth, back and forth. Vexation, a physical distaste for slimy water, sleepiness, fear that I wouldn't be able to unwind and sleep (which would weaken my work today), distrust of my own strength, the knowledge that the week stretches ahead of me, full of people, just when I need the solitude that provides the mental space and physical pacing that eases my work, the feeling of being frayed by demands tangent to my purposes—all these mental rats snarled and scurried, to be dispelled, finally, only by the effort of acceptance. A physical rhythm asserted itself. I went back and forth more easily. The water level dropped. By the time I walked slowly upstairs in the dark house, I felt quiet.

The plumber is fixing it now, whistling.

26 FEBRUARY

The newspaper this morning prominently displayed a photograph of a Cambodian man holding the naked, spraddled body of his just killed daughter. I place Sam's poached egg on toast, hot Ovaltine and honey in front of him. Bear daintily accepts his morning dog treat: a biscuit that comes in bony shapes attractive to dogs.

Superficially, a world presenting such disparities can only be comprehended within a logic of madness. Such a logic would have to be constructed, as indeed it has been, so well that remarkably few people revolt to seek new solutions. One of these is maladjustment to the world. I now see that when I left psychology I was even at that time refusing to aid and abet acquiescence to the premise that all was well with the world, that the individual's job is to arrange an appropriate stance toward it. Obviously, we have to make a reasonable adjustment. It behooves us to study the situation, to accept it pragmatically, to work within it—but, I think, with reservation. My own interest lies within this reservation, for within it we can accumulate experience with an open mind, and await elucidation. The accumulative process is fast in this civilization. The Cambodian child was killed yesterday. I see her dead today. Empathy invites a quick reaction: The whole world is a mad invention with no order, no sense, no hope of sanity. Yet the moon was setting this morning while I watched the sun rise. The air smells of earth and gently nudges my white curtains. I find myself in my accustomed position of paradox, with the responsibility for it.

Refusing to jump into the abyss of chaos, I return, as always, to order. I line us up: Sam, the dead Cambodian child, and me. First, we were all born, necessarily into bodies and hence into given situations. Forced into certain circumstances, we are forced to learn what those circumstances teach us. It seems that there is little choice here: Born, we learn. With a wary side glance at the fallacy of *post hoc propter hoc* reasoning, I press forward to the tentative conclusion that we are born in order to learn.

But if so, in what context? Here my Western mind hung for years and years, living out of dumb faith. And keeping faith, in some quixotic childish formulation, with Miss Perry and Mr. Lockhart, who remained set like Byzantine iconographic figures against the mosaic of my Easton childhood. Immovable, incontrovertible, inexplicable, they stubbornly asserted themselves in the background of my contemplations: one at her sewing machine, pale as death; the other stolid on his stool in front of his hardware store. As time spilled into my adulthood, one day following another until my own life was approximately the length of theirs when I had first seen them with my childish eyes, I began to perceive how for them also the days must have followed one another in some progression of meaning. Miss Perry made dresses for people: She followed the seasons—wool, cotton; and the events—denim, silk. Mr. Lockhart moved inside for winter; when spring came, he propped up rakes and hoes on either side of the stool on which he took his ease in the sun. Measured by the sheer passage of time, of seasons, their lives partook of its grand sweep. At least I could know this. And that they endured. To endure can be at best a triumph; at worst, it teaches. Beyond this stark understanding, I simply continued to hold them in some inviolate respect. When in my reading I came across the concept that a single life may be only one in a series of lives, and when I began to test this idea out as a working hypothesis, the intransigent disparity in human happiness that Miss Perry and Mr. Lockhart symbolized for me took on another dimension. Such lives, apparently so meager, could be thought of as hard lessons, springboards to further growth and to new richness.

Last night a poet presented me with a hypothetical situation. Madame X, a Frenchwoman who neither speaks nor reads English, hence cannot even understand any labels the work might have, and knows nothing in particular about art, walks into an exhibition of my work in Paris. What do I expect her to experience?

I replied that I did not *expect,* I *hoped.* What I hoped was that something in her experience would, in some unpredictable way, rise to meet the work. We then agreed that, faced with the fascinating problem of translating what we know with the just accessible parts of ourselves into the available physical terms, we simply do our best, leaving all result aside.

27 FEBRUARY

Three sculptures are well started and seem to be making themselves under my eyes. The paint is a creamy delight. Strained and restrained through a tiny Japanese sieve that has somehow survived from my Tokyo years, it spreads sensuously under my brush, which seems scarcely to touch it, serving only to transfer it to the wooden surface.

An artist I know has just suffered an emotional storm. The fear of losing control is realistic. It takes a spiral of energy to spin off art, or any sort of demanding work. Inside the spiral is a vacuum chute, and down is faster than up.

Real rudeness pokes out in front of a person like a cowcatcher. Its impact is brutal. Three people who visited my studio recently took for granted that their own artistic context was the only one possible. This assumption was so natural to them that it never for a second rippled with a vagrant doubt. They delivered their opinions as if from the reverberating halls of Zeus. They were taken aback when, asked what I thought of so-and-so's work, I said I didn't know and was waiting to see. I was equally dumbfounded when, at the end of twenty minutes or so of solemn gazing and pronouncements, one of them said how nice the work would look in marble.

1 MARCH

Yesterday at the Baltimore Museum of Art, I was given a series of documents relating to my exhibit. Among them were reviews.

For one reviewer, a white painting is a white painting is a white painting; she pointed out that white paintings were nothing new. A second took the same stance. Both dismissed the paintings as uninteresting. The third granted the work the grace of its own context, with a quality of understanding that eschews the jump to conclusion. This is the kind of review I like. I am not concerned with reviewers' judgments, yea or nay; they cannot deflect my course. What they can do, and this seems beyond my resistance, is hurt my general self, the supporting troops, so to speak, of my striking force. A fourth reviewer long ago made up his mind that my work is calm; he entombs it under this epitaph, with a faint sigh of boredom.

Another article was the sensitive outcome of an interview one sunny afternoon in my living room. It felt right to me that I had apparently said, "There's a small still center into which conception can arrive. And when it arrives, you make it welcome with your experience."

The series of articles that have made a teapot furor began with one entitled "White Paintings Fit for That Emperor," dated February 9th and written by a gentleman named R. P. Harriss for the *News American*. The museum installation of my exhibit is illustrated with four photographs: (1) a man staring down at a square white air-vent cover just to the right beneath a painting; (2) a vertical painting juxtaposed in a neat design with two vents covered with grids; (3) a detail of one of these grids; (4) a straight-on rectangle within a rectangle, a symmetrical photograph of one of the paintings with the caption "First (and Last) Impression: Splendid emptiness . . . total absence of picturization . . . reverberating nothingness." In addition, a black rectangular outline, captioned, "R. P. Harriss (white portrait)." And a larger rectangular space onto which Mr. Harriss invites his audience to project their thoughts. He further invites his taxpayer readers to send these thoughts to the mayor of Baltimore and to the members of the city council, "who vote the funds that enable the museum to provide such interesting exhibitions."

By the following Sunday, the folks had joined the frolic. The rallying cry was "Equal Time for Black Paintings." Two decorate the page. One is captioned "You Know Who (black portrait)" and the other "Black Painting—Attributed to Buggins, Experimental Period. See notes on the artist, below." And we do see notes on the hypothetical Buggins, as well as more about "Miss Pruitt" and "Miss Pruines." One reader had mailed Mr. Harriss his newspaper page of the previous week with all the paintings blacked in. Others had solemnly filled in his proffered rectangle with drawings of their own, and one had even written a poem with twenty-one lines.

On February 23rd, the third Sunday, Mr. Harriss brought out his big guns: "Let's Be Serious (But Not Stupid, Too)." His points, made in the Latin, *Primo, Secundo, Tertio,* are well taken: (1) The artist is free to paint what he pleases; (2) the artist runs a risk of not communicating in painting what Mr. Harriss considers to be "essentially white expanses of framed canvas"; (3) the museum director risks the loss of his municipal funds when the artist fails to communicate. The last point is extrapolated into a virtual threat and has an ugly ring. My guess is that it was at this point that the mayor of Baltimore telephoned the director of the museum to assure him of his support.

The museum has responded by extending the exhibit until March 16th. It gave me an odd feeling, as I drove away yesterday, to see the juxtaposition of my name and birthday on the announcement board in front of the museum, in the city where I was born.

2 MARCH

A cursory reading of Mr. Harriss's articles made me smile a little, as I would at anything ridiculous; and he was, within his context, successfully making my work ridiculous. My civility fell back in dismay, however, at the ugly thrust of his real hostility, backed by his snickering supporters. The blacking in of the photographed paintings frightens me, like murder.

I got accustomed to sneers in the sixties. I thought my hide had been toughened. But I think the opposite has happened. I am more vulnerable. In those days, I was just generally tougher.

But this morning, I feel clear. It didn't last long.

The tendency to complete a gestalt is so strong that it is surprising so many people have trouble finishing tasks. It just shows the inherent difficulty of getting anything physical accomplished. Matter is stubborn. Only dogged effort brings a concept into an arena in which it can demand the serious attention we give a challenge to our own physical selves. It is here that "conceptual art" tends to be, using Alexandra's adjective, "lame." The concept, remaining merely conceptual, falls short of the bite of physical presence. Just one step away is the debilitating idea that a concept is as forceful in its conception as in its realization.

I see that this might be considered an intelligent move. The world is cluttered with objects anyway. The ideas in my head are invariably more radiant than what is under my hand. But something puritanical and tough in me won't take that fence. The poem has to be written, the painting painted, the sculpture wrought. The beds have to be made, the food cooked, the dishes done, the clothes washed and ironed. Life just seems to me irremediably about coping with the physical.

8 MARCH

The current series of sculptures is finished. As I took my hand off the last one at 6:45 last evening, I felt like going on and on, making more. But the desire had a febrile echo. I was glad to wash my hair, have a very deep and very hot bath, and sit down in candlelight with my young crew around me digging into plates piled with spaghetti, cottage cheese, salad, French bread, with ice cream and hot, bubbly chocolate sauce to top it all off. I felt a little heavy after all this, glad it was dark and time for bed, glad the major strain of the studio work is over for a while.

It is peaceful to sit here in the morning sun and know that my sculptures are finished. Whatever happens now cannot change what has already happened to me in having made them or to them in having been made.

I am bone tired.

12 MARCH

I have been under more strain than I realized. The cold or flu I have been walking around with has now seized me. I was flattened yesterday and am only slightly better today.

The principal symptom is dizziness and I ask myself whether this relates to my mother's death, dizziness having been the first sign of her brain tumor. I now feel her death hard upon me. Her fifty-fourth birthday was September 11, 1941. She died on October 27, 1941, forty-six days later. My fifty-fourth birthday is March 16th; forty-six days later is May 2nd.

I feel astonished that I am as old as she was when she died. Do I know as much as she did, she who seemed to me to know so much and to be so at home with it? Am I that faded? Is my skin as transparent? Do I look as delicate as she did? As fragile? I am living what feels to me like a vigorous life inside a body undeniably as old as hers was. Yet my memory of her throws this feeling of my own vitality into question. Could I be deluding myself?

I feel lonely to outlive her. She had blazed the trail so far. I have been, without actually giving it much thought, following in her footsteps. I have relied on her companionship and feel freshly bereft. In the undertow of her death, I feel my own. Will I die with scarcely a backward glance, quite matter-of-factly, as she did?

15 MARCH

Tomorrow is my birthday. I lived more in hope last year at this time than I do now, enjoying an Indian summer of my lingering feeling from childhood that at any moment my life would coalesce, reveal itself to me in such a way as to render me automatically whole. The Corcoran exhibit lay just ahead; I was already preparing for it at the museum. My inner gyroscope was quivering with expectation. So much had happened to me that was new the previous year that I felt anything at all might lie just around the corner. Not so now.

OSSABAW ISLAND, GEORGIA

18 MARCH

Prospero rules this island. Ariel's magic airs beguile, flirt, and delight, diminishing into the dry, just barely audible touch of palmetto leaf on palmetto leaf. I am enchanted.

Sun slants through feathery gray hanging moss and

echoes in the hot, secret hearts of the unseen lethal snakes. Cattle, wild pigs, goats, raccoons, and adorable tiny donkeys wander at will. I spy the scut of a deer's tail and see a vulture eating a dead pig. White herons stalk the sloughs on the edges of which crabs go about their leisurely business on the hot black mud. Wild roads crisscross the island, each named in some legendary commemoration: Harry Hammock, Tom Creek and Little Tom Creek, Cane Patch Island. It's all been improvised, like America itself, casually invented.

23 MARCH

My schedule here is now as regular as it is at Yaddo. Last night we watched a film about bronze casting. In my absorption in my own technique, I tend to forget the marvelously intricate devices of traditional sculpture, the tender pleasures of modeling and the drama of casting.

In a discussion of our trade, one of the artists here said that she had concluded that most people have a social attitude toward art. She meant, she said, that they take it on the same level as anything else, bringing to bear on it roughly the same discrimination with which they choose, say, their curtains. Like hummingbirds, they dip into art, their vital energies absorbed by the effort to keep their wings going hard enough to hold themselves up as viable members of the society. Regarded from this point of view, two aspects of response to art that have always astonished me become perfectly understandable.

The first is my mystification that people seem able to bear so many kinds of artistic stimulation: They see a ballet in the afternoon and hear a concert at night, or go through three museums in one brisk morning. But if it's like walking through a department store, no particular psychological changes occur, no strain is felt. My second bafflement is their failure to be excited by quality. Again this is perfectly understandable if a generally complacent, judgmental attitude is taken for granted. Such people respond on their own level instead of on the level of the art. They take art into their experience the same way they note the weather, relating it to their convenience.

So perhaps the thrusting crowds at the museums are, on a slightly higher level, like people pushing into a spectacular sale, aiming to take advantage of what's offered. The conversation after such an experience might be analogous. "I got a good thick parka for only thirty dollars, a real bargain" is replaced by "I thought the bronzes more interesting than the early pottery." In the first case, a useful object has been picked up; in the second, an impression has immediately dried into a socially negotiable opinion.

I round once again into my preoccupation with values. Taken all in all, it does seem that the degree to which people are aware is the most handy yardstick for seeing where they stand. How closely have they held on to their capacity to know directly and in their own particular way? To what degree have they eschewed the preconceptions of social conditioning?

25 MARCH

I went down to the kitchen early this morning to pick up my thermos bottle of hot water, forgotten last night. Returning to my room past the doors of sleeping people, walking easily in my blue and white *yukata,* the weight of the thermos on my left arm was like one of my babies. We were so often alone like that, the only ones awake in a house full of people.

Born when I was thirty-four, after years of heartbreaking visits to fertility specialists, Alexandra's life was a miracle to me. She was with me all day every day until she was around eight months old, when I started teaching two mornings a week. I used this money to pay for a maid five mornings a week, giving me three in the studio. My time with her alone was so continuous, so little distracted, that no particular hours were more precious than any others.

The first child is apparently often more confident and self-reliant than succeeding children. This period of solitude with the mother must have something to do with this strength. It has a honeymoon quality of unexplored, open-ended pleasure. I was fortunate that Alexandra was born with regular habits of character; somewhat independent too. She fit into my life so smoothly that, by the time her needs were preempting my own, I had developed maternal muscles of unselfishness. She never made demands beyond my capacity to meet them easily; sometimes an effort, they were never a strain. And my joy in her presence was total.

I mostly remember carrying Mary, like the thermos bottle but a lot heavier, tucked on my hipbone while I went about my business. When she woke early in the morning, I would give her a bottle, prop her up in her baby carriage so she could look around at the world, and wheel her into my studio, at that time an annex off the kitchen. I would work quietly for an hour or two before the day actually began. It was in this silent companionship that I felt Mary's presence most strongly. She watched with beady eyes, always on the alert.

Sam was born in November 1960, six months after we returned from San Francisco to Washington, early in the coldest, snowiest winter I can ever remember. The freezing weather made us cozy together, Sam and me. I used the guest room, two steps and one room away from ours but within hearing distance, for Sam's nursery. There he lay peacefully in the well-used crib. Against one of the two large windows was a spacious white table, the one I now use for drawing. This was his bathing and changing place. Against the other window, placed so I could look out easily, was my nursery rocker.

When I heard his first tentative cry in the middle of the night, I used to get up instantly, turn my electric blanket on high so my bed would be warm on my return, slip into a bathrobe, and tiptoe quickly to his crib. I never turned on a light. Part of the magic closeness was the semi-darkness of the high-ceilinged room lit only by a street light. I would immediately turn him on his back so he would be happy knowing that he would soon be comfortable, fill and plug in the bottle warmer, put in the bottle brought up in the ice bucket the previous evening, change him (lovely warm water, nice dry double diaper), and wrap him in a soft knitted blanket. By this time, the bottle was just right. Then we would sit by the window, rocking gently, both warm and happy in a little world isolated by snow and sleeping people, rich with the homey smell of baby and milk.

It was in this familial context that, one year after Sam's birth, my work suddenly erupted into certainty. I was taken by surprise and to this day do not know why it happened.

When Sam was a few months old, fairly launched, I rented a room at 1506 Thirtieth Street, across from our house. On the third floor, looking west from a sort of turret that jutted out into the air, it was rather pokey but exceedingly convenient as I could run back and forth easily. I picked up my work where I had left off in San Francisco and continued to make loose drawings with black and brown ink. These were done very fast, on sheets of newsprint paper into which the ink was absorbed in such a way as to make them look more expressionistic than they were in my mind. I was on the track of square and rectangular shapes, articulated back into the depth of the ink, echoing the structures I had seen on archeological sites in Mexico, most particularly those of Mayan temples. I began making these obsessively repetitive shapes in the summer of 1958 after Mary's birth, not only in drawings but also in three dimensions. I used very dark brown clay, heavily grogged, and built up the sculptures from the inside out, using the classical method taught me by Alexander Giampietro. I still sometimes miss the marvelous feeling of rolling the clay between my fingers and thumb and then pushing the warm, full shape against its fellows to swell the unity of a structure growing slowly under my hand. This satisfaction with the certainty of a familiar and compatible process was one of the pleasures I had to forgo when my work changed direction and forced me to go against the grain of my own taste and training. On a visit to my studio early in 1961, Kenneth Noland pointed out to me the possibility of enlarging the scale of these sculptures. I remember my reluctance to absorb this idea, partly because I was afraid and partly because of my pleasure in using clay in a way that gave me such satisfaction. I think, however, that his suggestion opened up my thinking and combined with my obsessive concern with the weights of squares and rectangles to pave the way for the change that took place some months later.

The change itself was set off by a weekend trip to New York with my friend Mary Pinchot Meyer, in November 1961, almost one year to the day after Sam's birth. We went up on Saturday and spent the afternoon looking at art. This was my first concentrated exposure since 1957, when I had moved to San Francisco, and I was astonished to note the freedom with which materials of various sorts were being used. More specifically, how they were being *put to use*. That is, I noticed that the materials were used without particular attention to their intrinsic bent, as if what I had always thought of as their natural characteristics was being disregarded. For the first time, I grasped the fact that art could spring from concept, and medium could be in its service. I had always rooted myself in process, the thrust of my endeavor being to seek patiently and unremittingly how an idea would *emerge* from a material. My insight into the art I saw that afternoon reversed this emphasis, throwing the balance of meaning from material to idea. And this reversal released me from the limitations of material into the exhilarating arena of my own spirit.

At the Guggenheim Museum, I saw my first Ad Reinhardt. I was baffled by what looked to be an all black painting and enchanted when Mary pointed out the delicate changes in hue. I remember feeling a wave of gratitude—to her for showing me such an incredibly beautiful fact and to the painter for having made it to be seen. Farther along the museum's ramp, a painting constructed with wooden sticks and planes also caught my attention, setting off a kind of home feeling; I do not remember the artist's name but I liked his using plain old wood such as I had seen all my life in carpentry. And when we rounded into the lowest semi-circular gallery, I saw my first Barnett Newman, a universe of blue paint by which I was immediately ravished. My whole self lifted into it. "Enough" was my radiant feeling—for once in my life enough space, enough color. It seemed to me that I had never before been free. Even running in a field had not given me the same airy beautitude. I would not have believed it possible had I not seen it with my own eyes. Such openness wiped out with one swoop all my puny ideas. I staggered out into the street, intoxicated with freedom, lifted into a realm I had not dreamed could be caught into existence. I was completely taken by surprise, the more so as I had only earlier that day been thinking how I felt like a plowed field, my children all born, my life laid out; I saw myself stretched like brown earth in furrows, open to the sky, well planted, my life as a human being complete. My yearning for a family, my husband and my children, had been satisfied. I had looked for no more in the human sense and had felt content.

I went home early to Mary's mother's apartment, where we were staying, thinking I would sleep and absorb in self-forgetfulness the fullness of the day. Instead, I stayed up almost the whole night, sitting wakeful in the middle of my bed like a frog on a lily pad. Even three baths spaced through the night failed to still my mind, and at some time during these long hours I decided, hugging myself with determined delight, to make exactly what *I* wanted to make. The tip of balance from the physical to the conceptual in art had set me to thinking about my life in a whole new way. What did I *know*, I asked myself. What did I *love*? What was it that meant the very most to me inside my very own self? The fields and trees and fences and boards and lattices of my childhood rushed across my inner eye as if borne by a great, strong wind. I saw them all, detail and panorama, and my feeling for them welled up to sweep me into the knowledge that I could make them. I knew that that was exactly what I was going to do and how I was going to do it.

Mary Meyer and I returned to Washington the next day, and early Monday morning I bought some white shelf paper and went to my studio. There I drew to full size three 54" irregularly pointed boards, backed by two rectangular boards, placed on a flat rectangular board. I went straight down Thirtieth Street to a lumber store and ordered the boards cut to the size of my drawing; I bought clamps and glue and some white house paint. When the boards were ready, I glued them together, painted them, and there was my sculpture: *First*.

I returned immediately to the lumber store with two more drawings. While I was explaining to the man what I wanted and what I intended to do, he said mildly, "You can have them put together across the street if you want to, in our mill." "Oh, can I?" I said. "Thank you." And I seized my daughter Mary in her dark blue snowsuit from the counter where she had been perched to watch what was going on. I had to rush off for a carpool and hadn't time to go to the mill right then, but I remember stopping outside the store and going down on my knees in the snow to hug Mary and tell her that I could make whatever I wanted to now, overcome by the possibilities that surged into my mind. I had seen that size would be a problem and had had no idea how I was going to make what I saw in my mind in that little studio with my meager equipment, time, and strength.

When I got back to the mill, I went in to see the manager. He placidly looked at my roll of drawings and allowed as how he could make them up for me. But, he suggested, I could make scale drawings and that would be easier for us both. So off I went and bought a scale ruler. A young architectural student was buying something at the same time and showed me how to use it. So I set up a system: scale drawings and mill fabrication. I also telephoned the financial advisor who had charge of the money I had inherited and asked him to transfer five thousand dollars into a new, special checking account. I used this account exclusively for my work from then on, replenishing the funds from my capital without giving it too much thought.

In 1962, I made thirty-seven sculptures, ranging in size from that of the first fence up to around ten feet tall. Most of these I made in Kenneth Noland's studio in Twining Court, which he generously allowed me to rent for ten dollars a month after his departure for New York. It was a ramshackle old carriage house with a huge hayloft equipped with a large hay door and hooked lift, which I used to hoist the larger sculptures in and out. There were also four other rooms, two crammed with rusted bed-springs; I had these carted off, and then whitewashed one of the rooms so I had a place for finished work. No heat, no water, rats—I used to stamp my feet when I came in—and the place was dismally damp. No matter.

A large fever blister is spreading over my lower lip, the result of my carelessness last Sunday at the beach. It shakes me that I could forget that sunburn always makes my lips blister hideously, disfiguring me for at least two weeks. How could I forget? The fact leads me to the uncomfortable hypothesis that some part of me wants me to fail, to reveal my anxiety, actually to wave it like a flag. And just when I was hopeful that I could go through the schedule ahead of me equably. The fever blister will now almost inevitably accompany me as far as New York. Really, the waywardness of my weaknesses tires me.

While driving through the palm trees on the way back from the beach in Puerto Rico in January 1963, just a week or so before my first New York exhibit was due to open, I had a moment of purest panic. I saw clearly that I could have lain low, snug in my marriage and motherhood, and I most profoundly wished that I had. No one would have faulted me. There would not even have been much loss of face, as I had rarely let on that I was doing anything beyond being a housewife. As I eased the car over the sandy ruts, I thought to myself how pushy I had been in aiming to do anything more. It seemed incredible to me that in a short while I would have to face the public gaze. Every fiber shrank.

I feel something like that now. And I remember that I had a fever blister for the 1963 opening too. I dread the lecture at the

University of Maryland and the two exhibits. Maybe this feeling has to do with these weeks of shelter at Ossabaw. My mail has not been forwarded, or else has failed to arrive. I have had no touch with my regular life. I also dread the return to that life; my financial ebb is once again too low by far for peace of mind.

As we four women agreed at dinner in February, the idea that we, as women, have a right to protection, or at least the right to hope for it, dies hard. My scarifying fever blister embarrasses me, broadcasting the fact that I have not taken care of myself, making a bid for pity.

WASHINGTON, D.C.

I APRIL

My fever blister is now virtually an abscess. I have postponed the University of Maryland lecture.

2 APRIL

The financial roller coaster is, to speak plainly, a torture. It's all very well to regard the money to be received from the sale of Kenneth Noland's *Mandarin* as a legacy (one of my neater constructions, that), but the fact remains that in spending it I am spending capital. I will nonetheless have to ask André Emmerich for another advance on its sale to pay the income tax, and to pay living expenses as well. The dreadful feeling of draining bone marrow is returning. As if in a reversed telescope, as if I were dead, I look back at my comfortably secure strong body in my green and golden childhood.

My income tax seems to me astronomical. To the lady who helps me fill in the forms, my situation seems ordinary; she regards me as a small business just getting started and notes that every year I earn a little more. True, but never enough to stabilize into a modicum of security. I work as hard as I can, make the best decisions I can, and still sink into quicksand. André Emmerich, unfailingly sympathetic and practical, has made me another advance on the sale of *Mandarin*.

An underground art sheet in Washington accuses me and two other artists in town of clambering over our fellow artists to the top. How, I ask myself, have I ever climbed over anyone? I can think of no single instance in which I have put someone else down to my own benefit, nor of any in which I have been so put down myself.

The closest I have ever come to feeling bitter was at the end of the Corcoran retrospective last spring. One piece from the exhibit was sold—to a friend—and none from the Whitney. I found my work admired. Logically, practical support should have been forthcoming.

The New York exhibit opens in a few days. It's the old pitcher to the well again. My balance is markedly better. I step more firmly and pick my way more adroitly over the stones; I know when to move rapidly and when to slow down. But the pitcher is always a different size, shape, and weight; and the path is always unpredictably strewn.

After the opening of my first exhibit in New York in February 1963, an old friend asked me what had meant the most to me about it all. I remember collecting myself, knowing, and saying, "It's the only thing I ever did all by myself."

"But what about childbirth, having your children?" my friend gently countered, himself a little, I felt, shocked.

"But the children were James's too," I answered. And I told him what I had never talked about before: the intense cold of the studio, the lack of water, the Easter basket of painty brushes and bowls toted back and forth from home for washing, the rats, the bleak isolation of my studio in a dead-end alley.

The change in me between 1963 and 1975 lies in how my answer to his question has changed. It seems incredible to me now that I could have thought that I had done it all by myself. Incredible. The work flooded in beyond my volition; a very large number of people had helped me in crucial ways; and, although my inherited money had paid for the work, my husband had underwritten all the household expenses, keeping me financially secure, and, and, and. . . . I had been nipped into artisthood as inexorably as a sheep into a pen—who may well delude himself too that he is making decisions: right or left side of the sheep run?

My answer now would begin with gratitude. What means the most to me is that for some unknown reason I have been blessed (and I know now how rare that is, and how quixotic) to be able to make things that sometimes have meaning to somebody else.

The sculptures arrived yesterday in perfect condition. The little room at 41 East Fifty-seventh Street looks like a jewel box, neat as a Victorian lady would like it. But not as I like it. I intend to go in alone at the crack of the gallery's opening. I will take everything out of the room. I will then put one sculpture in, and another. I saw them there before I slept last night. The room is just plain too small. I will eliminate ruthlessly. This looks to me brutally suicidal from a financial point of view, André having conceived of this as a "bread and butter exhibit." Very well. I will teach, give up making sculpture, paint on canvas and, if further reduced, on paper.

It may be because it is so early in the morning—no coffee—that it looks so desperate. I am frightened. Somewhere out of my privileged past a resonance of confidence in being protected has continued to shield me: a fading echo of a now distant horn. Only a tiny piece of my being resists the spreading knowledge that I am rather slowly but very surely sinking into real financial need. I speak bravely of the children going to college, as indeed I intend that they will if they choose to. They take for granted that I will find a way for them to train themselves for their lives.

This exhibit, and the Pyramid one to come immediately thereafter, present me with a narrow twenty-degree-angle turn. It begins to seem to me inevitable that I will have to teach full-time (if I can find a job) and turn the main thrust of my effort into earning money. Given my physical and psychological weaknesses, this turn would, I think, kill the work inside me. But I must remember that it is early in the morning and that hope is an equal to faith and charity.

11 APRIL

The installation yesterday went poorly, by fits and starts. No sculpture seemed to choose its own place. But time has run out. It opens today.

I remember my easy stance on my last Emmerich exhibit in 1969, the nonchalant way I took in the whispered fact during the opening that so-and-so had bought such-and-such, and a certain person was even at that moment contemplating buying a certain other piece. I remember feeling a kind of surprise that I was being told at the opening, as it seemed to me rather immaterial. Not now.

But something more serious than personal anxiety is happening here. I believe that in some mysterious way my wish to sell, no matter how natural in view of my responsibilities, is harming the exhibit by my desiring more from it than that the work stand clear for its own sake. By wishing to sell the work, I am demeaning it and myself. The exhibit just doesn't look right to me, and I feel so unhappy in this position that I do not think I will ever again let this shadow fall on me or my work.

The fact is—and as always when I see a fact plainly I feel lightened, set free from the more or less conscious effort to maintain a delusion—that I cannot expect to earn a living from my work in art.

14 APRIL

The Pyramid installation is finished except for the lighting, which I shall do tonight. After returning from New York I straightened the house, had a hot bath, and drove down to the gallery. Eight sculptures awaited me there. I rapidly placed five in inevitable positions, eliminated three with a light wave, and departed expeditiously. It was the quickest installation I have ever done and I enjoyed doing it. My body is creaking like a wooden ship in a prolonged gale, but I am sailing well.

16 APRIL

The opening matched the installation: smooth. Sam and I drove down together. There were enough people but not too many. The air was fresh and cool. The effort people make to come to my openings never fails to touch me. Sam and I drove home peacefully. He made some pea soup, we had a little supper, and I went almost immediately to sleep.

18 APRIL

It appears that the University of Maryland is actually going to offer me a job. A curious turn of fate, that the state in which I was born arrives like the U.S. Cavalry to my rescue. And the Corcoran School of Art has asked me to teach next fall for a regular half day.

The *Arundel* exhibit at the Baltimore Museum of Art continues to elicit ire. John Canaday has sent R. P. Harriss a letter: "Dear Mr. Harriss [a blank page] Sincerely, John Canaday."

Proust once wrote that if he were dying and the sun made a patch of light on the floor, his spirit would rise in happiness. Within austerity there may, perhaps, fall a patch of light from some unimagined sun.

26 APRIL

The winter of 1933–34, when I was twelve and my parents were both sick, set a pattern for my behavior that I have not, I think, quite outgrown, nor may I ever.

I was so very much alone. Even before my mother went to the hospital in Baltimore, she abdicated a good deal to me and lay in bed, half-sick, half-well. The evenings were the worst. I used to check on her now and then, and bring her another hot-water bottle when she needed it. I remember one night she said, weeping a little, that I was a much better daughter to her than she had been to her mother. A little wave of conceit rose in me, but it was mighty little to put against the feeling of being forlorn and the knowledge that I was really not as competent as I was trying to seem.

Under this pressure, a certain crystallization took place in my character. Prematurely, forced by anxiety, it took on the rigidity of the unnatural. I accepted—I had to—the responsibility of being the caretaker, the strong one, and in doing so realized that I was behaving well. This made me egotistical and reinforced my attachment to the only method I had so far developed to handle crises, that of my mother's constructions.

A crust, so to speak, formed on my surface. It protected me from appearing afraid and from having to acknowledge my fear to the world. To whom, indeed, could I have acknowledged it? Who was there able enough to hear? But to hold this crust intact I had to deny fear to myself too, and this left me with crevasses of insecurity that in a more wholesome development would probably have been mere cracks.

On the positive side, I learned to rely on myself and to take the brunt without flattening under it. How long I could have done so, I do not know. The decision to send me and my young sisters to Aunt Nancy in Virginia for the summer of 1934, a summer that stretched to the fall of 1935, rescued me.

On Aunt Nancy's hilltop with Uncle Jim, who teased and laughed a lot, and their four children, I became, most thankfully, a member of a litter. Anonymous, I could rest in a warm mass of tumbling children, some older, some younger.

More than anyone I have ever known, Aunt Nancy knew how to make a child feel secure. To be near her was to be safe. Wise in the ways of comfort, she also had the knack of making work fun, and under her hand I learned how to swing easily from task to task, finishing each one and moving to the next without fuss.

My particular job was the milk separater. Every morning and every evening I put together the contraption; separated the milk by turning a handle fast or slowly, depending on thickness of the cream Aunt Nancy wanted; put the filled crocks in the old-fashioned wooden icebox; and washed the little gadgets, drying them carefully so all would be in order. My uncle would stroll through the kitchen and say teasingly,

"There's Miss Annie at her milk again," and I would feel happy. Aunt Nancy was great at putting up food for the winter, jars and jars and jars of peaches; we used to peel nine bushels a day during the peak season of the summer, and for this job we had special "peach dresses" (peach stains do not come out), put on clean in the morning and washed overnight so we could sweat them up the next day. Aunt Nancy even made her own soap.

In the evenings, which were always short because we went to bed early and got up early, Aunt Nancy would play the piano and we would sing. Or Uncle Jim would tell tall southern tales. It seemed to me that the family was unbelievably proliferated. There was always another new sweet-talking cousin or aunt driving up the hill to have tea, which we had in summer out on the lawn in a big, sprawling circle and in winter in front of a great fire. Aunt Nancy thought nothing of whipping up a couple of dozen delicious little cupcakes, which were all gone an hour later.

While she and Uncle Jim lived on their hill, I had a refuge. I remember telephoning her one morning in 1962 to ask if I could come down that day. "Uncle Jim and I will meet the train," she said cheerfully, no questions asked. It wasn't until we were driving into town two days later so I could catch the train back to my responsibilities that we even mentioned why I had come down. By that time I was able to speak without crying too much about what was making me unhappy. Aunt Nancy had no answers. She put me on the train and said to be sure to come back whenever I wanted to, but she had a massive heart attack shortly thereafter and died very quickly.

I have been working long hours in the garden during these spring days. The bushes are pruned, flower beds fertilized and mulched—a lovely soft brown field against which my little plants look, to my doting gardener's eye, charming. The strawberry plants are dotted with white flowers, soon to be delectable berries I can pick every morning for my summer bowls of fruit. The fig tree—known now for several years as "Mother's fig twig"—is actually taking hold. Last year it bore only one fig, which we ceremoniously divided into four pieces and solemnly ate though it was a bit sour as I had picked it too soon. This year Sam ironically predicts a "harvest."

30 APRIL

Signature stretched wide, then closed in on itself into one column in Daniel Brush's eye. This is precisely what I intended, though I cannot say how I hoped it would happen. Color occasionally just takes charge. The more I work with it, the less I seem to know about it and the more I trust it.

This is paradoxical but I can only say that for me it is true. A truth held, as so many are for me, on the symbol of Heraclitus's convex-concave curve unifying opposing forces. As I write, I wonder if the whole of my life wasn't set by this concept when I first heard it in Dr. Veltman's philosophy class at Bryn Mawr. My sculptures hold this line: the severe *logos* of structure magnetizing the flux of color. In life itself, it is love—I do not know anything else that unites so successfully—that is the *logos* magnetizing the myriad processes of life into radiant meaning. Love in this context being as simple as it can be when experienced most intimately, without intellectual or emotional elaboration.

Having taken off from the houses, trees, fences, and fields of my childhood in my work of late 1961, I very soon found that I was leaving the literal object behind. By simply going ahead with whatever presented itself to me in my inner eye, I discovered that what really interested me was proportion, which soon led me into the fascinating reaches of counterpoint between form and color, and ultimately to the work I am doing now, at once more austere in structure and more expressive in color.

The actual landscape, of course, remains, and I return to the Eastern Shore of Maryland now and then to look at it again. And at the houses in which I grew up. The first of these is owned by a friend, and when I visit her I can see once again, by scrunching down, the proportions that taught me as a child. The house was probably built about the middle of the eighteenth century and has never been remodeled in any way. But what I remember is clearer to me than what I see today. I go back and yet cannot go back. Time has locked it all away from me as if I had died. I am irremediably thrust into my own mind, and there I find it all, in weights and lines and colors distinctly my own. Just as in my work I found it was an essence rather than objects that held me, so I find it is only the abstract part of my experience that is real for me. I wander around the houses and gardens and see them with my physical eyes, while behind them glimmers the radiance of my vision. I have no home but me.

At dinner this evening the children laughed with me at the ridiculousness of my having spent nine hundred dollars to bring back sculpture I had spent nine hundred dollars to take up to New York to exhibit. We all caught on to the comedy of it and threw back our heads in wholehearted laughter over our dessert bowls. Bear loped happily around the table, tongue lolling, wanting to be in on the fun.

Sam is now definitely taller than I am. I noticed on an after-dinner walk that I have to look up at him if I want to be eye to eye. He rises on his toes when he walks, a habit that Mary Meyer, an acute judge of masculine character, always claimed marked interesting men. Bear circled around us, Sam looked down at me as he rocked up and down on his lithe toes, and I myself stepped out firmly in a more modest but just as happy way. The fruit trees have almost finished flowering and the lilacs are glorious. One of his friends, Sam said, recently contemplated hanging himself; another is in the hospital because someone stuck a knife in his back. Now, as I write, the night air is sweet and soon I will sleep, all ambiguities stilled within my fragile skull.

Yesterday I moved the houseplants outside to the terrace in the sun, the fish bowl in their dappled shade, and danced the hose sprinkler over them all. The oak leaves are slightly larger than squirrels' ears—just past corn-planting time in Virginia. A revel in my garden—wind, sun, dandelions, buttercups, and violets.

It was on just such days as these that I first began to know my father, during a bright spring when, apparently considered in some way ailing, I was made to lie in the sun a lot. My father would wrap me, still in a babyish one-piece cambric undergarment, in a steamer rug, round and round like a cocoon, and place me on a long chair on our brick terrace under the grapevine trellis. He would then settle himself next to me in the morning sunshine and keep me company. I don't remember that he read to me—though this was the Peter Rabbit era, and I adored hearing stories and seeing pictures; I just remember silence. A kind of meditative companionship that has always been most dear to me: profound unanimity.

8 MAY

I am informed by the University of Maryland that the funds for the job they had decided to offer me have been slashed by the state legislature. There is a slim chance that some rearrangement may be possible. I asked myself at 2:00 this morning, the dead hour of diurnal solstice, what we would live on this year, and had no answer except *Mandarin*, still unsold. My comfort is that I have done what I can to the limit of my ability in every way. I must move ahead now on faith.

17 MAY

André Emmerich has returned all my work except two small sculptures and two drawings. I like the feeling of tidiness, everything brought back under my roof, but the fact that there were no sales makes the recent exhibit in his gallery the most devastating defeat I have so far met. Devastating because I so need the money, not because I am unaccustomed to this kind of failure.

Wellington, when asked what he thought the most valuable characteristic of a general was, replied, "To know when to retreat and to have the courage to do it." I aim to retreat in good order.

20 MAY

It is now almost a year since the old woman in Arizona lay down to die. A man I washed for death years ago at Massachusetts General Hospital suddenly stretches naked under my eyes like a Caravaggio in the harsh light and shadow of his hospital room. He is still just breathing. Forty-odd, full-fleshed, smooth-skinned, dark-haired, a vigorous, competent-looking body. His wife, supported by their family, is waiting in the corridor. We, the nurse and I, wash him rapidly, racing the moment of death. He lies faceup, unconscious under our firm hands. We pull a clean sheet and a clean white ribbed spread over him. The nurse allows the sheet to cover his face. I fold it back as soon as I can without seeming to criticize her. We turn off the lights, leaving only one dim lamp in a corner of the room. I look back once as his family files into the room. The man is perfectly straight and flat and clean.

I see the woman curled on her side, dissolving into the desert detritus.

I feel a vague yearning today. At five this morning the air was already as palpable as deep water. It's the sort of day I do not particularly want to live through. But that part of myself that never stops working has plotted a summer of sculpture for me. Why, I wonder, does that part of me never give up?

Not that I don't rely on it. For years and years I was baffled by Cézanne's work. I grasped his principles and pored over the way he constructed his paintings and thought and thought about what he must have experienced to be able to put color down so that it expressed formal values in accord with his vision. But nothing did any good. I remained baffled. The paintings would swim into focus and then out before I could catch them whole. Until one afternoon at Long Lake in Michigan when, walking with Sam toddling along beside me in his little red-and-white seersucker shorts and red T-shirt, I glanced off to my right and saw a Cézanne—exactly as he would have painted it—in a curve of woods.

In thinking over the demeaned feeling left over from the recent Emmerich exhibit, I realize with gravity that I have, for all my care to try to do what is right, always wanted something out of my work beyond the making of it. It would be easy to say that I had lied to myself about this. Self-castigation is, like doing the right deed for the wrong reason, the most tempting of self-betrayals. The truth is at once cleaner and more humbling. I simply have not hitherto realized my own desires. In the sixties, I wanted to fly above, to command the air like a morning falcon. And, in the seventies, I have wanted to support my household. There's nothing inherently wrong, perhaps, in having secondary motives, but I do not like to have them.

I once watched a snake shed his skin. Discomfort apparently alternating with relief, he stretched and contracted, stretched and contracted, and slowly, slowly pushed himself out the front end of himself. His skin lay behind him, transparent. The writing of these notebooks has been like that for me.

4 JUNE

Spring is quickening into a scherzo, trumpeting the summer. The house, stripped bare for the hot days, is as open as a windblown shell on a beach. For a moment, I sit in it, content.

1978

New York. The East River surges past the New York Lying-In Hospital. In a dimension entirely different from the densities of steel and cement lining its progress on east and west, its waters move deliberately to and from the Atlantic Ocean.

I stand in a small white room beside a table on which my oldest child lies. Her belly is a mound of stretched skin, her belly button, stem of our common blood stream, is flattened to a disk. From smears of jelly on her stomach, two thin wires attach her to a black box. The doctor flicks a switch, and we hear an echo of the Malabar caves. "The baby's heartbeat is twice as fast as the mother's," the doctor remarks. The heartbeat is as impersonal in its rhythm as the river outside the window. The child's life is not as yet marked by human reliance on air. I am struck by a note of intent in the sound, as if I were listening to secret wisdom.

Alexandra and I leave the hospital and walk up and down

the streets of New York, happily stopping here and there to buy this or that for the baby. We walk arm in arm, close together—but not as close as my daughter is with her child.

WASHINGTON, D.C. Linked only the way yesterday is linked to the morning that rises around me as I write here in my studio, my life led to hers, as hers is now leading to her child's. Behind me *Portal*, a slim column, nine feet of pale, pale grays articulated just off white, looms in its packing. It is ready for shipment to Yaddo, where I will soon be going and where I will finish it. By analogy, I will then cut its umbilical cord and it will fall into place behind *First* and *Queen's Heritage, Landfall, Lea, Hardcastle*, and the other sculptures I have made, all synapses through which its life will have come into being.

I comfort myself with this construction, which has risen from my years as an artist, this fact of a continuing succession in my work that offsets a surprisingly bitter impression of having been cast aside. I am disoriented. My motherhood has been, I realize, central to my life as a stove is central to a household in the freeze of winter. I feel chilled. My sculptures are not my children. The construction of an analogy in no sense renders them alive. And I am accustomed to sustaining the effort of my work by offsetting it with the lovely affections of family life.

My mother was dead by the time I had my children. I have been moving for some months now, since the brilliantly sunny morning when we learned that Alexandra was pregnant, into uncharted territory. It so happened that Alexandra and I were alone on that day. We hugged one another in celebration and then came out here to the studio. I worked for a while, painting one light coat of color after another on a column. Alexandra sat on the studio step. We talked. We were quiet. Somehow, quite without emphasis, a new life joined ours.

Now Alexandra and her husband, Richard, have moved through a series of decisions to their present position: They wait in their white-painted, neat apartment for their baby. The crib and the tiny shirts and the pretty cotton blankets are ready. They wait, lovingly, for they know not what.

I know what. I look back over telescoped years. I am waiting for Alexandra's birth, and for Mary's, and for Sam's. I think of vaporizers and suddenly peaked temperatures, of fretful days and long, long hours in parks and of happinesses unexpected and unpredictable. Of prides and disappointments, of angers and joys, of calls on endurance that had to be invented as events demanded it. And of pain, the inevitable pain that marks the mother, peaking into a watershed that cuts off forever the playing fields of childhood. I weep for Alexandra's travail. I brace myself to meet, once again, the knowledge that I cannot take the suffering of my children on myself. That is the essence of motherhood. *Stabat mater*: Mothers can only stand.

My own aspirations fall into a new place. Once again, as at my mother's death, I feel my own mortality, but in my grandchild's birth transmuted into a kind of colorless immortality. Colorless in that it seems to bear no relation to the spirit. I am startled by this fact of the transmission of genes, struck for the first time that matter proliferates from generation to generation without regard for the personalities of the people involved. This new baby already has unimaginably innumerable ova or spermatozoa, some unknowable combination of Alexandra and Richard, of my husband and me, of Richard's parents, of unknown earthbound forebears. Depersonalized, we live on.

Now, I ask myself, what of the artist who has worked for so long? The steps up and down ladders, the wakings and the goings to sleep with my mind swinging with color, height, breadth, depth? I have only a modest answer: Certainly it does not become less real; certainly it continues. The scale, however, has in some critical way changed. A subtle crack between myself as artist and myself as human being worries me.

I find this situation humbling. I belong to this linked passage of life as unimportantly as the earthworm whose natural functions loosen the earth so that seeds can root easily.

The central emotional fact of my present state of mind—Alexandra's baby is due in about a week now—is not amenable to psychological ratiocination. Lodged like a dark bolus in my midriff is the certain knowledge that my daughter is going to suffer pain. She has never been in pain; she has never even really been sick. Her intact delicacy is like that of an apple blossom. She will be torn.

I turn for relief, for comfort, to my work.

NEW YORK. Richard telephoned this morning that Alexandra had just started labor, and I came right up here, returning to this hotel where, just a few weeks ago, Alexandra and I enjoyed a last visit to celebrate her coming delivery. I miss her. My last glimpse of her, as I turned the corner in a taxi on my way to the station, was as she stood, rounded in front, at the hotel entrance waving to the last second an immense bunch of lilacs and peonies she had bought to bring cheer to my room. When we meet again—some unknown number of hours from now—she will be flat in front and changed by mysterious alchemy.

No: Alexandra just telephoned. She is in her private room. I can go to see her.

She and Richard and I hung out the window of her room watching the boats skim up and down the East River. Her contractions came and went as easily. The river current reversed while we watched, the ocean churning back up into it in marvelously intricate, wind-teased textures, curled white against silky blue as in a Chinese embroidery. When the time came for me to leave, we parted with gaiety, exhilarated by a common hope.

Alexandra and Richard have a son. They all three did well. "Incredible" was Alexandra's adjective when she spoke to me on the telephone after the birth. "The baby was crying," she said, and in her voice I caught the unmistakable quiver of motherhood. Reassured, she handed the telephone to Richard and prepared to sleep. She is satisfied with herself; it was a job and she did it well. No fuss and feathers. Richard's voice had the same note of parental responsibility.

They now have a hostage to fortune. Never again will they lean on a window sill as they did yesterday afternoon watching boats on a sunny river, so wholly at their own command. Their son, yesterday *in* them, is now *beyond* them. Born, he cannot be protected, and they will never again be carefree.

When, later, I clasped Alexandra in my arms, we both cried a little. Reunited as if after a long, long separation, a journey on which she had gone to a far country. It was to her limit, she said. During the whole labor and delivery, she did not cry out. I asked her if she prayed. She said not really; but at one point toward the end she thought, "If there is any mercy . . ." and felt the presence of the Lord, quite matter-of-factly.

My very first feeling on looking at my grandson's face took me aback. It was as if neither of us were present, as if I for a second lost myself and couldn't find him in some ineffable void. No feeling of recognition or of his belonging to me in any way. As I came to, my first articulated feeling was actually one of respect for him.

YADDO. I am writing in my familiar Stone South studio. Behind me the windows open onto the mowed meadow, which smells as sweetly as always. The blackberry bushes are flourishing and the purple martin houses still stalk the apple trees. This time I have my columns with me, eight of them, three already under way. I am soothed by the routine of my work.

In a dreadful nightmare last night, I found myself thinking. "Oh, this is *real*. I can *feel* this texture. I am *alive* here." A thin, thin thread held me to sanity, and with the utmost effort I finally managed to cry out. I awoke in my familiar turret with "ma ma" strangled in my throat.

It is this that Alexandra has undertaken: a tie so powerful as to elicit a cry for help to a person long dead from a person fifty-seven years old, herself a mother and grandmother.

My drive to and from the University of Maryland, where I have been teaching since the fall of 1975, cuts through one of the poorest areas of Washington. One afternoon this year as I was coming home through the fading afternoon light, my eye fell on a man sitting in an aluminum-and-plastic chair on the front stoop of a drab apartment house: slumped, old, with one leg bound in bandages almost to the groin and stuck stiffly out like a pole on a slant to the cement; beside him a Pepsi can. Some resigned tilt of his head took me directly back to the wards of Massachusetts General Hospital, and all of a sudden it flashed across my mind that I had taken a wrong turn when I left the direct alleviation of pain implicit in psychological work and nursing. I saw my life as self-indulgent, full of willful delights. As I sailed past him in my car to my comfortable house and the prospect of a good hot dinner in my son's company—to the wide, varied landscape of my life—my heart contracted. What could my work ever mean to this man? A kind touch of my hand in a moment of fear or pain would have been more in his service than the endeavor of my whole lifetime.

This incontrovertible fact stuck in my craw for weeks and weeks. That area of my drive to and from work became charged with the man's presence; on rainy days I regretted that he would not be there; on fair ones I looked for him.

For a long period, he failed to appear at all, and I thought perhaps he had died. But one day he was there again and I was glad. The bandages had shrunk; he had a cane. By the end of the term, I saw him less frequently. I like to think he is now going about his business, but he remains in my mind, central to my thoughts about my life.

And to my recognition of limitation. In the range of my character at any given moment, I have acted in the only way it seemed to me that I could have acted. This in no way means that I have done what was right; only what was possible for me. Sometimes I have done what I knew was wrong, and have rationalized. But rationalization is a form of desperation. It takes kindness to forgive oneself for one's life.

In the narrowest meaning of the concept, it is touch, after all, that I am after in my work: the touch of my hand I hope to find transmuted into something that touches the spirit. I hold the structure neutral: a column. Painted into color, this wooden structure is rendered virtually immaterial. The color itself is thus set free into space and into the ever-moving sun, which marks time. And color is the least material of matter: vibration as light. A touch.

The most demanding part of living a lifetime as an artist is the strict discipline of forcing oneself to work steadfastly along the nerve of one's own most intimate sensitivity. As in any profession, facility develops. In most this is a decided advantage, and so it is with the actual facture of art; I notice with interest that my hand is more deft, lighter, as I grow more experienced. But I find that I have to resist the temptation to fall into the same kind of pleasurable relaxation I once enjoyed with clay. I have in some subtle sense to fight my hand if I am to grow along the reaches of my nerve.

And here I find myself faced with two fears. The first is simply that of the unknown—I cannot know where my nerve is going until I venture along it. The second is less sharp but more permeating: the logical knowledge that the nerve of any given individual is as limited as the individual. Under its own law, it may just naturally run out. If this happens, the artist does best, it seems to me, to fall silent. But by now the habit of work is so ingrained in me that I do not know if I could bear that silence.

JULY

Alexandra and Richard, whom I have just visited in New York, are deepening in character. This change—Sammy was born one month ago—is marked in all sorts of infinitely touching ways. Some of them are familiar. Years ago Alexandra draped a scarf over a lamp in her room so Rose Primrose's kittens could sleep undisturbed; the other evening, as we left the baby peacefully asleep in his crib, she threw another scarf over another lamp with the nonchalance and grace of an habitual gesture. Her routine for bathing her son is a delight. She puts in the tub a small inflatable yellow raft marked "Tubby." In this the baby floats happily while she washes him all over with her hands, gently and leisurely, chatting to him in a lively lilt. She then splashes out the water and, turning on the faucet, gives him a sprinkling shower, turning him over on his stomach at some point so that his head and arms dangle off the soft round "Tubby" rim. There he can turn his head about and wave his arms and kick in the sprinkle, sometimes against her palm so he springs up and down as if jumping.

I had forgotten how sensuous babies are—all skin and touch and need—and how central to their care is one's own sensuality. To watch this reciprocity between Alexandra and her baby, having rejoiced in it myself, gives me happiness for my daughter.

She and Richard are not, of course, getting enough sleep. And there are the inevitable rubs as a selflessness that can never be quite as natural as selfishness develops into habit. But in the evening, as we sat in the hot dusk, we felt content as families must have for millennia uncounted.

The new balance my children's maturity is bringing to my life makes me wonder about the differences that seem to be surfacing between the artist in me and the mother. The artist struggles to hold the strict position she has found keeps her work to a line she values, while the mother is trying to grow by adjusting to the rapidly changing conditions my children present me as they move out on what seems to my schematic mind a sharply rising trajectory: They are learning a great deal about a great many aspects of life very fast. What they apparently expect from me is a point of view. They ask questions and they want what answers I can give. The artist's answers are only rarely useful to them. And the positions from which they ask are often different from those I have been in myself, so I have to use my imagination to empathize. This is taxing. At the same time I must maintain a center in myself so that what I say is honest. In order to do this, I have to examine and reexamine my own experience and apply it as best I can, inevitably at an angle oblique to theirs. What I am finding is that the artist is too strait and too self-centered, too idiosyncratic, and that the mother is not as useful as she once was. She is too nearsighted and wishes the children to remain within arm's reach. I am wondering now if some third person—who is neither artist nor mother, as yet unknown, unnameable—has developed behind my back. Perhaps the person whose first feeling when she saw her grandson's face was respect? If so, her mode of being is tentative.

SEPTEMBER

The pangs of labor are a metaphor for the startlingly painful and difficult process by which a child is delivered into adulthood. The curve of physical motherhood peaks over the watershed of labor into a shining Shenandoah, a broad valley that seems to new parents to stretch forever. For me it had the same smiling lavishness as the first days of delicately greening marriage: a lovely open space with brown-furrowed fields snugly bounded by ramparts of love on either side. It never forcefully occurred to me that the children would scramble up these very mountains out of the valley to see what lay beyond. Paradoxically, the more hospitable the valley, the more energetically they climb. The end of parenthood is implicit in its beginning: separation.

The first birth is documented. A doctor stands by; physical facts are readily available; literature abounds in accounts of birth. Folk knowledge hammocks the pregnant woman: she sways in a gentle wind of attention.

Not so with the second birth into adulthood. That is a solitary business for the parent. The course of events is not documented—cannot be, as each child tears the connective tissue differently. The process cannot be examined in advance and prepared for with specificity. One child of mine had her first menstrual period for two days without telling me; when tears came into my eyes at the news, she was astonished. It had seemed to her her own business, as of course it did to me once I had grasped this fact clearly enough to honor it. But a needle had by that time painfully pierced the amniotic sac in which I had, all unknowingly, been carrying my daughter. Another child appeared to become more and more indifferent to me. Instead of chatting—and we are a chatting family—the child turned laconic. I was lucky to be told, "Good morning." Until I recognized this cutting off for what it was, I thought the child surly. Another simply ran in and out of my heart as if it were a drafty old barn with doors creaking in a desultory wind; only straw and shelter were needed.

The increasing independence of the child has to be met and matched by an increasing independence of the parent. I have found no other way to render this separation healthy for all of us. And it has seemed to me that, since I am the parent, the burden of foresight and consideration lies squarely on my heart and intelligence. Yet all of us, my children and I, work to regroup, they as much as I. One difference in our efforts lies in the fact that nature is on their side; they are naturally invigorated by their opening into the excitements and fascinations of adulthood. I, on the other hand, have to accept diminishment. This has been a little frightening. I thought at first that habitual patterns of feeling and thought, no longer nourished by daily give and take, would have to atrophy entirely, that my Shenandoah would dry up into sand-stormed desolation. The landscape has indeed changed, but slowly and subtly. I homestead the valley. I tend. My children live, either physically or metaphorically, elsewhere. Occasionally it is lonely. I wander now and then, hearing the echoes of their voices.

But—and in this I have been blessed—the ramparts of the valley have never hemmed me in. I have often rejoiced to climb out, to look back lovingly and to return faithfully, steadfastly, and trustingly. I have only had to give a child a hand now and then over a hummock or up a scarp over my own tracks. The change I have had to make in myself is in the act of faith required to place my hand in one of theirs and my feet on their newly discovered paths, no matter how rocky and perilous they have seemed to me. Awkwardly, stumbling, trying not to point out (too often) my own well-trodden and cherished ways, I have earnestly tried, slowly—I need more time than they do; a reluctance of the heart persists stubbornly, inaccessible to reason—to trust their surefootedness. And my reward is that I have found myself set free to move farther than I had hitherto dared, my own freedom widened to the degree I have been able to confirm theirs.

It is the artist who reaps this reward, justly enough, as it is she who has climbed most often up the ramparts to see what lay on the other side. And it is she who has a real understanding—cross-grained as she is in relation to society in general—of the passion for independence that motivates my children. Yes, yes, she thinks, while the mother clutches a teddy bear in some dim cave of a nursery; yes, yes, they need to go as I have always needed to go. And, yes, I want them to climb up and out; I am curious to see what they will do and how they will do it. The artist rejoices that her studio is a fact; she already has what she needs as much as her children could ever need anything they may find in their lives. It daunts the mother that the artist is so indifferent to the children's departure. Yet it is to the artist that the mother turns for relief as the car drives off bearing its cargo of phonograph, records, books, carefully pressed clothes, extra tidbits of money, and arms waving from every window. It is the artist who hurries the mother through the house cleaning after the departure and then forgets her as coolly as she waved farewell to the children, returning to her work, solitary, engaged.

It is becoming apparent to me that the mother and the artist do not speak much to each other, and when they do the speech is initiated by the artist who wishes to be off about her business. She chivies the mother to get herself time. Otherwise, she views her as a source of knowledge, but of knowledge already assimilated—and here it occurs to me that the artist is giving the mother short shrift in a way that strikes me at this moment as rude. She is hurting the mother's feelings as surely as the children occasionally do, and with a lot less justification. The artist could not have come into herself without the mother's experience: she owes her a debt of honor for all the layers and layers of hourly, daily, weekly, monthly, yearly knowledge of what life is. For the artist has grown out of that rich ground as surely as she has grown out of the student, the wife, the nurse, the friend. The fact that the mother is bothersome, takes up the artist's time with her demands, in no way reduces this fundamental reliance on her wisdom. The artist also is more dependent on the mother than she likes to acknowledge, set as she is on her independence, for just as the mother turns to the artist for comfort so does the artist turn to the mother for nurture when her work gets her down. And the mother never turns her off curtly. Rather, she rushes in with nourishing soup, hot baths, and a tender hushing into night.

Yet a change is taking place—took place, I am beginning to believe—in that moment when I recognized in myself a new "I" who respected my grandson. I feel her as I write. She stands clear in a new dimension. She sees that the artist has already claimed the territory granted her by the departure of the children. With an objectivity untainted by pity, she observes the mother crouching over the family hearth and notices signs that the old habits of motherhood are beginning to pall; she foresees a time when they will become vestigial.

She sees, for example, that it is my reasonable obedience to my children that has gradually become a launching pad for them. In no way does this imply moral abdication on my part. On the contrary, my consent to their guidance confirms their moral fortitude as it expands the context of my own. Certain points have set the arcs for this slow change, which is in a fundamental way not so much a change as a development of my early determination to honor my children. When Alexandra and Richard brought their newly born son from the hospital, I wanted very much to be there in their apartment waiting to welcome them all. Alexandra explained that Richard wanted to drive them home and settle them in alone, and that she agreed. They would telephone me, she said, when they were ready for me to come over. My feelings were hurt. I had a vision of warming their household. I obeyed, and we had a meeting at once peaceful and joyful, and only as I write do I realize that my presence in a welcoming role would have been an intrusion into their marriage—and a not unusual one at that: Generosity is often the stalking horse of control.

WASHINGTON, D.C. Our dog Bear died two days ago. I can see his grave from my studio as I write. He lies, head to the east and feet to the north, near the Japanese weeping cherry tree; just beyond the reach of his paws I have planted a spring-blooming pink camellia with palest yellow and white jonquil bulbs encircling it. He died beside my bed, within reach of my hand, where he had slept for most of the nights of his life. I woke early that morning, made sure he was lying peacefully on his side on a soft quilt covered with Mary's purple knitted shawl, and then lay down myself for a period of quiet before beginning the day. When I rose, I went around the bed to him. He had just that moment died. I closed his eyes, wrapped him carefully, and carried him downstairs to the garden. I had forgotten how difficult it is to die. The spirit is so ingrained in the body, its lightness palpable only in its negative effect: Bear's body was much, much heavier when I carried him downstairs dead than when I had carried him upstairs alive the night before.

I watch and listen for him, sadly.

The image of death on a galloping horse is apt: it overtakes, scythes what is meandering along at an ordinary, daily step. Violently or delicately wielded, the scythe blade is itself clean and silent. The act—dying—is intact. "A final tenderness," Aleksis Rannit writes. And one that shares with all tenderness the confirmation of individuality.

OCTOBER

On the night of October 5th the telephone rang. Already in bed, I reached for it rather absentmindedly. A deliberate, female voice asked if this were Mrs. Anne Truitt. I said, "Yes." "This is Suburban Hospital. Your son has been in an automobile accident." I saw Sam's white shirttails hanging down the back of his jeans as, just a short time ago, he had turned out the door with, "See you later, Mom," over his shoulder, off with a friend to pick up another for a study session at his school. The upper reaches of my head seemed to elongate. Some inner silence opened. My body began to hum with energy.

"Is he hurt?" I asked.

"We are evaluating him."

"Is he dead?"

"He's conscious." The woman's voice changed so abruptly to a note of hope when she said, "He's conscious," that I realized instantly he was badly hurt.

"Is he dying?"

"We are evaluating him. He's conscious. He gave me your number."

Again the note of hope.

I repeated, "Is he badly hurt?"

She said, "We don't know yet. We're evaluating him." Evaluating—I took in the word, thinking carefully about something being valuable.

"Where is the hospital?" She began to give me directions and, in one of those serendipities that mark life, its appearance and location flashed like a color photograph in my inner eye; I had casually gone there some ten years ago to visit a sick acquaintance. I stopped her. "I know exactly where it is," I said, and asked her to call Sam's doctor. She said Sam had given her both names, his doctor's as well as mine. My heart lifted a little. Intelligent boy, I thought, taking good care of himself. An inner lock slipped smoothly into place and my bond with my son Sam became abruptly whole, as it had been before he was born. Through this placental connection I began to feel, and into it I began to pour energy.

The woman on the telephone was asking me questions about insurance. I was glad to answer. The questions slowed the action; I felt it incumbent on me to be "normal." I asked her please to tell Sam that I was on my way. She warned me to drive carefully; the rainstorm—indeed a tempest—was causing a lot of accidents. I said I would be careful, and I was. Careful—and fast. I parked at a rather sharper angle than perfect, ran toward the emergency-room door, stopped myself so I would not be out of breath, and was glad I had when I was confronted by a pair of cool eyes that evaluated *me*. I carefully outlined my insurance credentials. She offered me a cup of strong black coffee, very hot. I held it in my two hands and drank obediently, exchanging enough words to reassure my telephone friend. A final clear look, a very slight nod of her head. "Yes," she said, "you can see him."

I carefully dropped my empty coffee cup into a waste-basket and walked through swinging doors into a narrow hall. Sam and his two friends lay on stretchers, and I took in with a glance the fact that the friends were all right, both wide-eyed and alert. Sam, pale, bloody about the face and neck, was attached to an intravenous bottle. He lay inert, eyes closed, under a coarse sheet; on a shelf under him was a pile of cut-off clothes, splotched with blood; his glasses also, intact by chance. When I spoke to him, placing my hand firmly on his shoulder, he opened his eyes, blurred with pain, but conscious. "Hello, Mom." I spoke to him in commonplace reassurance, rather briskly than sympathetically, in the tone with which I had said "uh-oh" when he had fallen as a toddler, as if this were only another in a long series of mishaps with which we had dealt efficiently. "It's my back," he said, moving a little.

"Can you move your toes?" I asked. He twitched them, and relief flooded me. "It hurts," he said without self-pity, rather as if surprised. "Yes," I said, "we'll have to see what's wrong and fix you up." And I patted him gently, as he had patted me eons ago when he had first nursed right after his birth. "How are Robert and Brad? How are they?" He twisted anxiously in an effort to see the other stretchers, which lay some distance around a turn in the emergency hall.

"They're all right. I'll go and see them. Lie still."

And I moved to the other boys, first to the one who had been driving, whose head was bandaged. His eyes full of tears, he gazed at me with infinite grief. "Is Sam all right? Is Sam all right? I thought he was killed."

"No," I said, "not at all. He's going to be all right." The

third boy was cut about the face but calm. A plastic surgeon was already on his way, I was told. The parents had been notified, and their school—one of the boys was a boarder.

A neurosurgeon had seen Sam; an orthopedic surgeon had been called; a trauma specialist had already checked him and given orders. A nurse hovered over him. He was due for X-rays. There was no way to check his injuries until that was done. By the time he went off for the X-rays, the other parents and the headmaster of his school had arrived. The plastic surgeon got to work on one of the boys and stayed to sew up Sam's neck and face. By that time he had been X-rayed. A broken pelvis, internal injuries of unknown extent. The neurosurgeon stayed on call. The trauma specialist returned to look at him. No water, no medication for pain because of the possibility of brain damage or of extensive internal injuries that might need an immediate operation. Sam twisted and turned with pain, I was relieved to see. No paralysis. And no whining. He endured well. He was going to be able to walk; no spinal injury as far as they could tell. I began to draw deeper breaths and to ask for blankets: the boys were cold. Slowly, facts settled. The two other boys were able to go home. Sam was admitted to the hospital and, by the grace of God, into a room otherwise unoccupied, so I could spend the night with him, an infraction of the rules for which I was infinitely grateful. He slept on and off. The nurses checked him frequently for neurological damage. I stood by his bed, looking down at him, one hand on his shoulder, one on his leg, as if to keep him safe. I watched through a blurring rain the flashing lights out on the highway. The dawn finally lightened the sky.

A gray day. A nurse brought me some coffee. All the signs were positive. No operation would be necessary. I must go home, I was told. He had stabilized.

For an hour or so yesterday I was truly convinced that it was impossible to do everything that had to be done: a visit to the doctor with Sam, leading to return visits and to future visits to other doctors; trays to be carried up and down stairs as he is still in bed much of the time; pills to be doled out at proper times for both of us—Sam for pain, me for a lingering infection. My desk was horrifying: slithers of brochures and letters (some unopened) and art magazines and art announcements and requests for information and Christmas orders; immediately looming letters to be written for my work at the university; details of scheduling, planning. But before I went to bed last night my desk was cleared, resulting in a pile of stamped letters on the front hall table, and a bulging brown paper bag of trash in the kitchen.

We have recently been discussing the "problems of women in art" in my seminar class at the University of Maryland. Not an academic question for this group. One student is a grandmother. Four are mothers. One has three sons launched into college. Another has seven children ranging in age from three to fifteen; another three children—twelve, thirteen, fifteen. Another three women are conscientious wives.

One of these students is the second I have taught in the last three years who is trying to use childbirth as the subject matter of her painting. The first concentrated on the vagina widened into a birth canal between the struts of the legs. She repeated this image in black ink on thirty-six-inch rolls of heavy brown paper in an attempt to render it cogent. Somewhere along the line, despite her earnest efforts, the specific image dissolved as she became increasingly involved in the act of painting on its own terms.

The current student paints the whole body of the woman: head foreshortened by perspective at the top, toes curled almost around the edge of the canvas at the bottom, huge hands clasping a just born baby on a distended stomach, vagina loosened. She has made only one of these direct works so far. Her husband is made nervous by it, she tells me. Of course. Any sensitive man would suffer to see so exposed—and by herself—a woman he had lovingly taken into his arms and to whom he had entrusted for cherishing the future of his body as she had entrusted hers to him. The paradox of the most tenderly creative union possible between two human beings leading, in the nature of the act itself, to the pain and blood of childbirth lays bare our condition. We are enmeshed in dilemma. Each action initiates a contravening reaction. A man, most loving, brings a woman to agony. A woman, most loving, brings herself to pain.

Yet these facts, emotionally powerful enough to suggest potential for an art equally moving, evade specific expression.

Sam was hurt three weeks ago today. It is as if the ocean floor of my being had erupted and all my waters had been disturbed. We all felt the quake, but in the other members of the family the waves have subsided. Sam himself is crutching around cheerfully. A piece of glass in his neck is something added; a tooth is something missing. My mind is moving in that loose way these days, as if unhinged: "Something old, something new," silly catch phrases. I feel aquiver. My span of attention is short. I try to think but keep circling back to the fact that Sam's body, once perfectly whole, is now broken. His pelvis is mending but will be forever crooked; not enough to show but out of alignment. Like my sculptures, he went out into the world and got broken, but I cannot mend him as I can them. I move uneasily in a new dimension of helplessness. The artist is no comfort to the mother here. I glance out the kitchen window at my studio as if it were invisible.

NOVEMBER

Sam is recovering. For the past twenty-four hours I have felt him mending, his proportions coming into proper order. Some shrill, carking note that has been jangling us both stopped last night. The relief is as keen as that felt when a wailing baby is put to the breast. My proportions, too, are slipping back into place, and I am on an even keel again for the first time since the accident. The uterine cramps that have been intermittent since October 5th are decreasing, have stopped almost entirely. This reaction strikes me as bizarre, but, since it is true, I have necessarily to recognize its reality. It is as if I had to take Sam back into the uterus to protect him, to reestablish the placental connection in order to nourish him through his crisis. Perhaps because of this primitive reaction, his recovery is marked by an increasing independence for both of us, a feeling of health and ease as if, in some mysterious way, he had accomplished his second birth, into adulthood, by means of this violent accident.

1979

MARCH

To wake up crying is unnerving. Unnerving is perhaps the word for my fifty-eighth year of life, which ends in two days: unnerved as in unhorsed.

Yesterday in my seminar class, we studied James Joyce's *Portrait of the Artist as a Young Man*. At the end of our discussion, I read aloud the last sentence, "Old father, old artificer, stand me now and ever in good stead," and heard my voice break. It is that nerve that is failing me. The hopeful part of myself, which has been able to express so little of what that hope portends. For it was a dream of love between man and woman from which I woke up crying this morning. When I meet in dreams this man whom I loved, I always know that he will leave without a backward glance, but I always have a painful question: Will he bother to say good-bye? Last night he did: He turned back from the laughing voices calling him off to a car with its engine already idling. In the darkness, we stood close and looked into one another's eyes more simply than ever before. We kissed solemnly and then he drew me to him. I put my head on his shoulder and for one-two-three seconds allowed myself to rest. The sort of shudder children make to end a storm of sobs moved my body against his. We both knew better than to acknowledge it. We looked once more (he is kind this time, I thought) and then he turned and went, and in the flick of his body dismissed me. I stepped back toward my house. And I am going to be fifty-eight, I thought, walking straight into waking.

The nerve of my work has not failed. *Second Requiem* is in progress. *Lighthouse* is clearly on the line. Plus two sculptures that will go into a New York exhibit projected for 1980. I have had to spend capital to make this work, an iron decision. But I have always been appalled to notice how terrifyingly determined the artist in me is. That spearhead of myself advances at full charge while the camp caretakers crouch behind bushes.

The S.S. *Penland,* Cunard line, was a small ship, my mother remarked with just perceptible disdain. My sisters were eight; I was ten. We were on our way to England for a summer with our English cousins. One morning I woke in the upper berth to find my father bustling cheerfully below. Myself, I felt sick and scared. My berth twisted up and down and then side to side and then, without quite turning over, up and down again. My father helped me over the high wooden rail. "Up you get, Annie. Up you get and up we go on deck. Hurry up, hurry up. . . ." By this time I was trying with weak fingers to button the tiny pearl buttons on a pink cotton dress. "Don't bother with buttons. Just come on, come on."

He thrust a coat on me, everything every which way, socks and shoes and out into the narrow, hot, salt-smelling corridor. Holding me firmly in a pawlike grip, he opened my mother's door and said that he was taking me up on deck. "All right, Duncan." My mother was sleepy. I felt better. We would scarcely sink while Mother slept. My father shoved me along, up steps and through heavy steel doors and finally over the high threshold of a final door and out onto the deck.

A light gray-blue sky and a darker gray-green sea, heaving in humps now delicately articulated outlines above my eye level, now surfaces fretted by windy scatterings of raindrops and lacings of foam. "Keep your eye on the horizon," said my father firmly. "You'll be fine in a minute." The wind picked me up instantly. My feet rooted on the deck, I hung onto the rounded wooden rail and rode up and down in a world that suited me perfectly. The ship was in a proper proportion to the sea, which met the sky on its own terms: Where the sea ended the sky began, and where the sky ended the sea began. For the very first time in my life, I felt at home. "Right," was my thought—as it was to be thirty years later when I rounded the Guggenheim Museum ramp and caught my breath at the grand space of Barnett Newman's painting.

APRIL

My cousin Nancy, first born and most lively of my generation of the family, was buried yesterday. On just such a day of sun and breezes she was married. I see her in her gauzy wedding dress sitting on a striped lawn chair in front of Aunt

Nancy's white clapboard house, under the spreading summer oaks, fortifying herself for the ceremony with a peanut butter sandwich and a tall glass of milk. Her first baby died. She lost another by miscarriage after she heard that her husband had been killed at Anzio.

Though time is immediately chafing, we owe to it the amplitude and delicacy of our interior landscapes as we age. Particular memories enhance these inner reaches, which seemed to me yesterday imbued with a mystery within which the ugly can of my cousin's ashes could with grace be let down into the red Virginia earth, the color of her once vivid copper hair.

A lecture today at the university on Mōtonōbu's panel paintings for the Daisin-in Daitōkuji in Kyōto left me adrift, wrack on a haunting sorrow.

Approached by a pebbled path, the Daisin-in is modest, as befits a Zen temple. Inside, the very dark wooden floors shine, rubbed by the immemorial slip-slip of felt-clad feet. To my stockinged soles, it felt cool, indifferent; an indifference rendered poignant by the storied garden of stone. The abbot recites the tale: A baby turtle leaves his mother and wends his way in perilous life. He is a small rock, fathered and mothered by rocks, surrounded by rocks. All is dry. He swims in a river of stones winding between the ancient temple walls. The passage into maturity is turbulent yet, the raked pebbles suggest, limited. The turtle has grown; he is a larger stone now. He moves toward the dark barrier that is the main corridor of the temple, under which the river of stone flows. We who listen are entranced. The turtle is real to us. The abbot smiles and smiles while he recites the tale. I heard him myself, twice, and he repeats in the same way the same words, each one as hard as one of the stones of which he speaks. He smiles, but I am crying quietly. I am in the strait, rigid rocks of maturity. I am dry in a dry place. We move across the corridor. My heart beats and I hide my tears: We are *gaijin*, foreigners. We do not belong here. Is the abbot's smile malicious? Yes, a little. But he leads us over the shining corridor and tells us that the turtle has made it through into the perfectly proportioned, immense space of the main garden in which his rock is blissfully dwarfed. The struggle of birth, youth, maturity—all narrow passages—are behind him. He comes to rest at the roots of a fruit tree. In its bloom he is set free into the fresh, moist air, into some ineffable spring for which I yearn.

For all that I felt myself dry in a dry place in Japan, it was there that I managed to get my moral feet under me; that is, to line up my life in accordance with the principles I had always held dear and to which I had not always up until that time been able to adhere. Not that I always do so now, but the years of reflection in Japan, isolated as I was, cleared the underbrush out from under my weaknesses so that they stood clear and I could begin to protect myself from them. Guilt is, I think, one of the "enemies of promise," though I do not remember Cyril Connolly noting it as such. If the artist is not at moral ease, energy goes into conscious or unconscious rationalizations that are betrayed in an inability to maintain a consistent philosophical key. This failure, however subtle, undermines the trust implicit in the placement of oneself in an artist's hands, and it is precisely this relinquishment of self that permits the impersonal enhancement that is one of the gratifications and enlightenments of art. Yet, no matter what efforts we make, we have no guarantee of moral vision; I have often done what turned out to be wrong while believing with all my heart and mind that what I was doing was good.

When Alexandra and her son, now nine months old, walked toward me at the airport, I was delightfully taken aback by their presence. Imagination is, after all, feeble. Our days are moving now to the baby's rhythm and to the cadence of comfortable talk with a trusted daughter whose experience begins to parallel mine but has all the provocative interest of being her own. The house sings with sunshine, lilies, flowering branches, narcissi, daisies, breezes, and Sammy's breathy chug-chugs, which precede his appearance on all fours and echo after his round diapered rump as he churns off. Early this morning I sat at my kitchen table hemming a calico tablecloth, Sammy beside me in his high chair, gnawing on an apple stick. Familiar, I thought, as I have thought so often during this visit—the smells and noises and concerns and delights of a baby. But not perfectly familiar. When my own babies were this age, I do not remember giving in so to their rhythms. It is not that I have less to do; I have, in fact, more. But when I am with my grandson, I care less about what I have to do, abandon myself more generously to the simple pleasure of being with him.

In some curious way difficult to put my finger on, my generation of women suffer from a subtle sorrow that stiffens us against just such abandonment to the pleasures of the moment. A legacy, perhaps, from the Victorian rigidity that in America bypassed the Edwardian frivolity and descended to us in the form of standards precluding pagan joy. Many of us have been lonely too, deprived by our male peers of that sensitivity they had to brutalize out of themselves in order to undergo the Second World War. Confronted by the probability of their own deaths, it seems to me that many of the most percipient men of my generation killed off those parts of themselves that were most vulnerable to pain, and thus lost forever a delicacy of feeling on which intimacy depends. To a less tragic extent, we women also had to harden ourselves and stood to lose with them the vulnerability that is one of the guardians of the human spirit.

MAY

A kaleidoscopic trip to New York. Alexandra and Richard's apartment is altogether charming. Very patterned: photographs; paintings; drawings; gay multiprinted cloths on chairs, sofas, and pillows; mohair throws; plants. I had had my doubts about taking care of a baby in New York, but they evaporated in the sunshine of Central Park: We could have been in a Vermont orchard, trees in flower all around us, the city muted.

Mary had fresh flowers in "my" little room of her tiny apartment, which is strewn with books, posters, and punctuated by the tinkle of the beads hanging on doorknobs—the hallmark of Mary's habitations. She drew me a hot bath in the tub, which stands on claw feet in her kitchen. I drifted off to sleep against the comfortable background of her voice on the telephone with a friend. Surely one of the unexpected delights of parenthood is the reversal of being put to bed by a child.

Alex Castro, master printer and owner of the Hollow Press, and I are choosing paper for the lithographs we are preparing to make together. As we go through samples of "white," I am reminded of a psychological experiment at Bryn Mawr for which I was a subject-observer for a whole year, one hour two or three times a week. I sat in a dark room looking at two small illuminated disks. My job was to discriminate between "brightness" and "lightness" and to define equivalents. An exquisitely calibrated training for my own particular sensitivity in art.

I am enjoying the process of lithography, partly because of the pleasure of working with Alex and his assistant, Caroline Orser, and partly because of the relationship I feel with the Bavarian stone on which I work—my first touch on stone since the fifties. And partly because of the fascination of reversing an image—seeing the weight change from right to left pivot on an imagined balance. Mixing the color is fun, has a sort of lighthearted quality because Alex and I work on it together in consultation; I am not at all accustomed to talking about my work as I make it, and find that I take an unexpected delight in a communal effort. We work in the Piranesi space of the press, a disproportionate volume of air above in a great warehouse, a random geometry of packing boxes and various presses enclosing us as we hover over the lithographic press itself. Alex turns its creaky, stubborn wheel, which groans as it revolves; Caroline pulls the print. We look, say a few words, and move on, united in an excitement we play down. We have not yet made a print we recognize as the *bon à tirer* (the master print of fine enough quality that an edition of prints can be pulled from it). As we sweated companionably one recent afternoon, Alex looked at me over the stone and remarked that some people never know this profound pleasure of work for its own sake. They work only to live.

The other night at the high point of an attack of pain, a blinker in the dark of my mind flashed the sentence, "My father wouldn't like me to suffer like this." Last night at dinner someone remarked on the beauty of Mother's portrait, which hangs in my dining room, and I felt a loss as poignant as a scent. Today as I walked along the street between my doctor's and my lawyer's offices, I suddenly missed my parents with all the forlorn longing of a lost child. In the sudden sting of tears, I realized that a buoyancy I have had all my life seems to be departing. Certain hopes, innocently flowering like little primroses under the larger bushes of my expectations, are quietly drying up. I passed a model of a huge BOAC plane—the sort of thing I ordinarily like to examine and imagine myself in: What seat would I choose? What would I eat?—with only a glance of indifferent recognition. It begins to seep into my mind that I may never be going anywhere on that kind of plane.

I am, however, going to the studio, where I am about to use on a sculpture a color-glazing technique I devised for drawings in Tokyo in 1966. With it I hope to catch a transparency I have tried to get in my sculpture since 1963. For all my efforts in that direction, it just never occurred to me to try this particular way until the other morning when all of a sudden I saw how it just might work. I am afraid though. If it fails—and it depends on a very light, sure hand—I will be once again stricken. So I hover over the column, already undercoated, and fritter, let my timing slip until lack of time justifies lack of resolution.

Well, yesterday I stopped hovering. My hands were perfectly sure and steady, rendering my earlier trepidation irrelevant. Yet it remained in the atmosphere, and as Sam and I walked back into the house from the studio I asked him—for the first time, as I almost never ask what people think of my work—what he felt about the sculptures we had just been moving around. Discomforted, he looked a little embarrassed and then said that he had never understood what I was doing. "Do you mean," I asked, "that you have never over all these years understood anything at all about what I was trying to do in my work?" and began to laugh, startled into hilarity that Sam and I had been living on such parallel lines. But his look of relief went straight to my heart even as we both laughed, peels of affectionate understanding of misunderstanding echoing in the living room. Sam allowed as how he did not understand art at all, in a kindly way, and went off to play in a tennis tournament. How sweet he has been all these years, hefting my work around so patiently, all the while perplexed. My conscience smites me. A natural reticence keeps me quiet about my work, but I am distressed to have made the kind of high-handed assumption about my very own son that I try so hard never to make about people in general. I have unwittingly insulted him by treating him as a nonperson while using his strength for my own purposes, and I am ashamed.

Daunted too. Painty fingernailed, hair skewed up on my head, wearing Alexandra's discarded maternity dress (Richard said it was too ugly for her), I am working long hours, and the artist is for once assuaged. But, at the cost of such misunderstanding, the price of these hours is too high. I have been neglectful. As my children, particularly now Sam as he verges on manhood, begin to live increasingly complex inner lives, I will have to be at more pains to discriminate inflections in my experience that might be useful to them—and then take the time to talk about them. As I think about this, I pick up heart, contemplating a way leading out of the old habits of my life and into a new kind of exchange with my children. I have begun to notice how carefully they watch now to see if I am competent. They mark my decisions and relish for me every action I take that renders me independent from them. I feel them waiting for me to relinquish some hold on them, which seems to come down to a kind of sadness that enfeebles them. When I give up this sadness, they will be relieved. But I cannot rush. I have to live through and out of this place in which the mother keeps wandering in the empty, twilit nursery.

But Sam would, I think, like to talk to the artist and she would—now that she was focused on him—like to talk to him.

Hadrian on the Emperor Trajan: "As soon as the weary emperor had reached Charax he had gone to sit on the shore, looking out over the brackish waters of the Persian Gulf. This was still the period when he felt no sort of doubt of victory, but for the first time the immensity of the world overwhelmed him, and the feeling of age, and those limits which circumscribe us all. Great tears rolled down the cheeks of the man ever deemed incapable of weeping. The supreme commander who had borne the Roman eagles to hitherto unexplored shores knew now that he would never embark upon that sea so long in his thoughts: India, Bactria, the whole of that vague East which had intoxicated him from afar, would continue to be for him only names and dreams. On the very next day bad news forced him to turn back. Each time, in my turn, that destiny has denied me my wish I have remembered those tears shed that evening on a distant shore by an old man who, perhaps for the first time, was confronting his own life face to face." (Marguerite Yourcenar. *Memoirs of Hadrian.* New York: Farrar, Straus, and Young, 1954, p. 90.) As must all of us who live long enough to see that we cannot make the ends of our aspirations and our achievements meet.

AUGUST

My house and garden are orderly, without ripple so early in the morning. Fresh water began to sluice into this quiet pond of my establishment when Alexandra and her son returned yesterday. Sam arrives this evening. Mary and all her possessions—she travels like a Bedouin—are due in on Tuesday, and the next day we all leave for a week at the beach, where Richard will join us.

BETHANY BEACH, DELAWARE. A family vacation is a pressure cooker. We are all hotted up as we try to balance ourselves into some new version of the unit we used to be when the children were indeed children and not young adults. Our very affection for one another is a bother. We get in each other's way trying to be helpful, and our family habits are obsolete. When we arrived at the beach, I galvanized the "children" to settle in immediately, make beds and lists and arrangements. These arrangements were—I realized instantly when I woke up this morning, rested—out of whack as far as I was concerned. So in the predawn I peacefully reduced my territory, pulling my personal things back into my single room and the half-bathroom. In some similar way, as peacefully if I can, I must reduce my territory in the lives of these people most dear to me in the world.

The children must have had a conference after I had gone to bed. They announced an expansion of their territory before I had a chance to declare a shrinkage of mine: They undertook all the work. This, they said, looming around me while little Sammy played with pots and pans at my feet, was my vacation. We would be independent for breakfast and lunch; they would do dinner. They watched a little anxiously: Was I going to accept their generosity or reject it, a reaction that would have announced a troublesome possessiveness of my role as mother? Relief all round when I thanked them.

A lovely vacation. Sunrises and sunsets on the beach, a wild storm through which we walked to return contentedly to hot tea, jigsaw puzzles, and P. G. Wodehouse read aloud; Hesiod to keep me company and jaunts at night for everyone except Sammy and me, who go to bed at roughly the same time. Not much real conversation. It was as if we called a tacit moratorium on all that lies unspoken among us.

WASHINGTON, D.C. Now we are disbanding. Alexandra and her family left for New York from the beach, all folded neatly into their little Volkswagen. Mary and Sam and I drove back here for the few days that remain before their departures— Mary to Paris for a year abroad, Sam to his first year of college.

Sam leaves this morning. His effects have disappeared into a dilapidated canvas duffel bag, which looks like a snake that has swallowed an elephant. He is sleeping. I heard him moving about restlessly during the night. We did our final errands yesterday afternoon and, with mutual relief, agreed to a reading dinner. I ate at the kitchen table and read Ruth Beebe Hill's *Hanta Yo*. In the Totowan tribe (whom the new Americans named the Sioux), no boy looks his mother in the eye or speaks to her directly after the age of ten. I told Sam this as we drove about yesterday, and he took the point instantly. We are both socially daunted to be parting. A ritual is lacking, yet we feel his departure a rite of passage. I had thought to mark it with a celebratory dinner, but neither of us could rise to it. We took the Totowan way, modified to a neutral companionship.

Sam is often more sensible than I. I was making conversation on the way to the airport when he said abruptly, "I don't want to talk about this kind of thing, but if you have something serious to say, I'd like to hear it." So I spoke a little. And though what I said sounded to me tinny—I felt flurried—he listened, and we parted neatly. I looked briefly at his seer-sucker back and drove away. All sorts of escapes from the vacuum he left behind him fluttered in my mind—I could go to the National Gallery, visit a friend, get a detective story from the public library. Then the image of my studio slanted across my inner eye, and by the time Sam's plane took off I was working and my "Godspeed" rose silently under the sander's mechanical skirl.

SEPTEMBER

I am spending long, slow hours lingering over the launder-ing of Mary's multicolored scarves, all of which run and have to be hand-washed; I iron them on both sides as if in smoothing them I could smooth the way of our separation. It doesn't do much good. I keep thinking of the cold Atlantic Ocean. But of all my children Mary most fiercely retains her initiative, as I have myself, and I am determined to honor her enterprise. No Totowan way for us. We chat and laugh and scurry around. When we fall silent, we feel one another in the house as if we were trying out what it will be like when she is really gone and only our feeling of connection will remain.

Mary left for France yesterday.

I write the sentence and stop. I feel stopped. Since the spring afternoon in 1955, when the doctor telephoned to tell me that I was pregnant, until yesterday at 1:30 p.m., a complex wheel of ever more complex wheels within wheels, some untoothed by time, some newly minted, has turned day and night. At one low point yesterday, while Mary was upstairs prodding her possessions into her bags, I lay on my flowered sofa in the sun, contemplated my future without the more or less daily company of my children, and felt utterly bereft. As if all sound and air had been sucked out of my atmosphere. I got up, took Mary out to lunch and out to the airport, and we both managed to smile, even to laugh, as we waved cheerfully. Some of me, though, I left on the sofa and she lies there yet, stare-eyed and still.

Storm and trouble. Paris is almost as easy to reach by telephone as New York, and over that great distance Mary and I have been discussing her astonishing decision to turn right around and come back.

Mary landed in New York last night. I do not know why. I do know that she would never have made such a drastic reversal without good reason, which she will tell me about when the time comes. She is settled back into Sarah Lawrence College and into some new faith in herself and her judgment, which she mysteriously found in Paris.

I can't help being happy that she is back.

OCTOBER

Waking into night a few hours ago, I placed my left hand, as if to soothe myself back to sleep, on my breast. I glanced down and in the dim light I saw as well as felt my gold wedding ring. All in a second, a confusion of senses both kinaesthetic and temporal, as I have not worn that ring since 1969.

I am wondering about the feeling, akin to a wasting illness, that is overwhelming my vitality. A sort of postpuerperal reaction, aftermath of the second birth of my children? Some unnameable loss seems to have occurred to my body itself, some scooping of tissue and blood that has left me weakened and weeping without sound. Am I, in that gesture of placing my hand on my breast to soothe myself back to sleep, substituting my own body for the lost bodies of my babies?

In the end, short of death, the body carries the day in any conflict with the spirit, clutching it cell by cell in a grip as unremitting as that of Heracles holding on to Proteus. It does not actually matter what I am thinking or feeling. My body turns under the stars as naturally as the dirt to which it will return. My doctor knows this better than I. On his instructions, I am lying in the sun. Yesterday, under the brilliant Indian Summer sky, I lay drowsy, idly waving away the fat bees that were buzzing over my ripening figs, and inside my lolling body I felt a little spot of health, like a drop of Greek honey, begin slowly to swell.

I have trouble expressing my feelings in all these passages about the second births of my children without sounding to myself declamatory. The years and years of minutes invested in the person of a child pull, second by second. And they only pull, tender as hairs. They do not break. There is no natural end. Yet as I write I hear the cry of wild geese in the lemon dawn. Below them, the sun-slatted earth; their feathers filled with air, magnetized to a mark in the southland. Who would not rejoice in their free flight?

The sadness of parting with my children has nothing to do with the cant of "wanting to be needed." I do feel needed, and it is precisely because I do that I am so surprised by the depth of my feelings of separation.

We have been discussing photography in our seminar. My students look at artifacts as habitually as I read. They take it as much for granted that a significant part of their experience consists of reproductions of visual reality as I that a significant part of mine consists of printed reactions to experience; just as they take for granted air invaded by indifferent music.

I wonder whether my students' senses are not actually different from mine. I overload so much faster than they do. Could it be that my baseline of stimulation at birth in 1921 in a small country town renders me incapable of adjusting easily to a range of visual and aural impact fifty-eight years later? The curve of environmental stimulation from 1921 to 1979 is steep, right straight up. Recalling my childhood, I hear birds, leaves in wind, human voices, the crumple of paper, the fall of beans in a barrel, barks, miaows, and occasionally horses' hooves clip-clopping. That is not much sound, to take that modality. Most of my students began to live around 1960. Muzak already filled public buildings, and what is to me the painful rasp of the mechanical television voice threaded the daily life of householders. To compound this aural repletion with the visual, add televised images. Newsstands sprout and fill with flamboyant magazines; the pages of these magazines riffle and flutter. In the silent houses of my childhood: *Harper's,* the *Atlantic Monthly,* and the *New York Times*—none of them with pictures, as I remember. Pictures were either paintings hung on walls or reproduced in my storybooks—Maxfield Parrish, N. C. Wyeth, Arthur Rackham, Kate Greenaway, Beatrix Potter—and they were special: out of the ordinary and invested with the power to evoke all that my imagination had already added to the stories they illustrated.

It may be that the relative silence and the almost wholly natural visual world of my childhood (blurred by myopia) renders me especially sensitive for the entirely logical reason that my sensory thresholds were set unusually low. What other people do not see at all can look to me not only perfectly plain but also too much, heavy, overemphatic. Since in my work I have struggled to adhere honestly in all strictness to my own sensitivity, the work may indeed tend toward the imperceptible.

In this light, the reception of my work is no mystery.

NOVEMBER

Yesterday restless, restless. As troubled as the yellow leaves that never quite lie down on the still-green grass outside my studio window. For the very first time in my memory, I felt angry while I was touching the paint because it moved wrong. "My hand is off," I thought, and then, "I'll just keep on and *force* it." This is a not unfamiliar situation—sometimes I find my hand simply cranky. Determination can lift it into competence if not grace. And so it was yesterday, though I was careful to stop short of the critical coats leading to the final, very delicate glazes, which require so much more than mere determination. I strained and bottled the paint for that particular sculpture, scrubbed my sink to give myself a break, and then steeled myself to go on with the undercoats of two more columns, watching warily that the beat of their coming into being did not fibrillate out of cycle with their rhythm. "Who will use all this paint?" I mocked myself, gazing at my legions of color, feeling jangled. I fled as twilight fell over us all—leaves, grass, and the sculptures, which continued just to stand there, mutely demanding.

I sat at my typewriter grimly. My mind took over like a dancing bear. I finished off two pieces of university work. It was full dark. The house was cold. A hot bath failed to soothe. I finished a book while I listlessly consumed a silly, unbalanced supper. I took the November *Arts* to bed, thinking to knock it off so I can lend it to one of my students. I expected neither to be instructed nor moved—too jumpy to be either. I had only just enough resolution to force my dancing bear through a few more hoops. Before decently folding myself into sleep, I reflected dully that artists often lie behind on the field long after the art combine, the broad-bladed harvester of informed criticism, has mowed, bailed, and stored the crop.

"Once the realization is accepted that even between the closest human beings infinite distances continue to exist, a wonderful living side by side can grow up, if they succeed in loving the distance between them which makes it possible for each to see the other whole against the sky." (Rainer Maria Rilke, *Letters: 1910–1926*. Quoted in a letter to Mary on her wedding day.)

1980

JANUARY

The "forest" of sculptures that André Emmerich is showing in his gallery this spring is standing in my studio. John Gossage photographed it yesterday while I sat in my one studio chair with its blue-and-white Yukata material pillow.

John told me that while he was photographing in Seattle his eye, wandering over the landscape, was caught, moved on (he was thinking, "That's a nothing photograph"), then moved abruptly back to settle on two telegraph lines intersecting at a precisely "right" point. He photographed them. The point of intersection and the lines themselves were, he said, those of the *Arundel* paintings. I mentioned what Eleanor Munro had said about the *Arundels*: that she had seen such intersecting trajectories before—traces made by particles in a cloud chamber. I have never seen a cloud chamber, and I wonder if artists occasionally pick up a range of actual physical fact beyond ordinary sensory reach.

I walked through the "American Luminist" exhibit at the National Gallery as if coming home. I had not known that I had been so lonely. Boston harbor scenes: the clipper ships of my ancestors could have been among those masts. Mountains strongly peaked and valleyed, close as grass to a child's eye, far as sky. Noble icebergs for the mermaids of my dreams. The sea itself, scimitar of light. And the innocent sunsets of my childhood, forthright splendors. I stumbled from painting to painting, room to room, and gazed, enchanted, astonished. A quotation from Emerson displayed on a wall: "The health of the eye seems to demand a horizon. We are never tired, so long as we can see far enough." It is for the health of the eye that I eschew formal changes that harness attention into thought.

I find myself a wholly ardent latter-day luminist—and that despite the unevenness of the paintings, their occasional garishness, failed taste, awkwardness, and a jarring note of self-conscious pomposity. As steeped in American landscape as they, heir to the American transcendentalism I drew in with my mother's milk, I find a little place here among people with my turn of mind. Artists who use landscape as an armature for light, as I use abstract structure. Artists who wish to set the light free, which is what I also wish to do, to make it visible for its own sake.

Mary is here on a quick visit. We are enjoying ourselves immensely, ranging happily from our personal lives to James Joyce to Prince Genji to Tolstoy. Fresh spring peas drop from their translucent pods into my earthenware bowl; the iron clumps on the ironing board. We breathe in the crisp smell of freshly pressed cloth in the sunshine. Mary drinks apple juice full of nourishing pulp that we feel sure is welcomed by her growing baby, a silent third in our lively conversation. Mary remarks on the fact that all of Tolstoy's characters are sustained by their work: Anna turns to her desk, Karenin to his business, Levin to his fields, Kitty to her household. The final price for Vronsky's waywardness is that he is deprived of his work. We agree that work is the backbone of a properly conducted life, serving at once to give it shape and to hold it up. Of like mind, industrious by nature, we work even as we talk.

NEW YORK. This morning I go to André Emmerich's gallery for the installation of the "forest" he has wanted to make of my sculpture ever since 1963. Do I feel excited? Yes. But dispassionate. I watch the sea gulls cross and crisscross the island of Manhattan from the East River to the Hudson, casually endowing the city with the perspective of irrelevance. It is this kind of distance that marks off this exhibit from my past exhibits in New York. I see it as a minor event in the history of the André Emmerich Gallery, a significant event among others of interest in mine.

WASHINGTON, D.C. The young sculptor who had invited me to the Provincetown Arts Center and was shepherding me through my schedule last week gave me lunch in his studio and then suggested that he depart and I lie down for a few minutes to rest before my next critique. Prone under his

Hudson Bay Company blanket, I looked up into a white space lined with shelves on which his sculptures stood. Turning my head, I saw larger pieces and power tools and sawdust and wooden staves, all the paraphernalia of work. Unexpected tears spilled slowly down my cheeks. I saw clearly that I had given this up, this freedom of the artist's life lived entirely in the studio. In the early fifties I could have chosen it at the price of leaving my husband; I could have smashed the context of my life in which this married state was set, pronged on little golden fingers like the diamond and rubies in the ring my mother gave me on my eighteenth birthday. My character, which pivots on a passion for clarity, held me to a line that led me to pay other prices for other prizes, to let this particular fierce joy slip past me.

On reflection, by right. My character, which I now experience as pivoted, developed out of a flighty youth. Intense, hardworking, but given to ill-considered darts and forays. Without the steady discipline my husband and children provided, I might have frittered my energies on the edges of my aspirations.

MAY

The spring is advancing into summer with relentless, orderly steps too rapid for my winter-set mind. It is as if I do not wish to be disturbed in the dim room of my adjustment to solitude. Yet, in that dim room I made sculptures of more brilliant color than I have ever before. I simply do not understand how this could be. I have been flooded with color on the inside, drab on the outside. I am tired and would, left to myself, stop the spring right here and lie down with the violets on my lawn. But habit is very strong and I have instead been cleaning the house all day. Now everything is in place, what you see and what you do not see. New summer pillows in the living room look fresh against my cool flowered slipcovers. My curtains are crisp from my iron. The tidy, soap-smelling linen closet alone is enough to give me a modicum of peace. It is interesting that things in themselves good—things usually pejoratively called chores—are so good for you, reliable healers of a reluctant spirit.

JUNE

NEW YORK. Mary's son was born early this morning. After hearing the news, I lay back in the predawn dark and, as the tide of happiness receded, I saw that it had pulled out on some long, bare inner shoreline of myself and had made the slope glisten for the last time: Both my daughters are now mothers and in the proper nature of things more mothers of their children than they are daughters of their mother.

When I am here, within the circle of my family, I feel reluctant to leave it. A seductive ease enfolds me, a wanton abandonment to younger and stronger hands. A hint of comradeship with the furtive apology that occasionally refracts behind the eyes of old people—I am weak, I will make trouble for you, you have to wait for me—mars this ease, though very little. I follow Sammy, who runs around Central Park as if it were his own kingdom, with affectionate eyes; he now uses words a lot and we all aid and abet him, but some of me is sorry when social sounds replace silence. Alexandra and Richard are expecting another baby. I rub my daughter's back and do her dishes and sweep her kitchen floor and read Beatrix Potter's *Jeremy Fisher* to my grandson. I have also been cleaning Mary's apartment so she and her husband can bring their baby home to order. She is looking serene and fresh. We have chatty suppers in her hospital room. I note with interest that my new grandson is already within these few days losing the intense and indomitable individuality of the newly born, the stamp of which only begins mysteriously to reappear in a middle-aged face. He will have to earn his character now.

JULY

WASHINGTON, D.C. I have been having a difficult time in the studio. The riot and revelry of early summer and the excitement of another grandchild's birth with another on the way have elicited in me an unusually generalized feeling of creativeness. Perhaps the mother, damped down, revolted and actually tried to step into the studio. In any case, I have had another bout with that part of myself that so overwhelmingly wishes to pour emotion into paint, to get it out so that it looks as powerful as it feels.

There are artists who have this gift, but I am not one of them. This seems to be a fact I have to learn over and over again. I have actually had to strip paint off a sculpture—for the first time since the years in Japan. For a period, *Monk's Way* stood bare, until all of a sudden, and without any volition on my part other than a determination to wait for it, color flooded into it and locked into place as if it had always been there. While this was going on, *Antipode*, released in some way by my acceptance once again of my limitations, simply stepped forth: wide color suspended on the four corners of the column from visible strands of lightly brushed paint.

One of the fascinations of being an artist is living in all the dimensions of life with an artist inside you. An intractable and always mysterious companion—but companion is the wrong word, as the artist does not care at all about companionability. Mine doesn't anyway. She is as stubborn as a mule, I sometimes think, and she can leave me lonely—as she just did when she refused me the release of expressing myself, held herself aloof, and then took matters into her own hands.

Last night at dinner with a group of people in their twenties, I felt now and then the way Aunt Nancy used occasionally to look when she visited James and me toward the end of her life: at a loss. The loss is adaptability, I think, and the resulting inelasticity is sinister. A shift as distinct as one within a spectrum of color has lengthened the distance between me and the world around me. The distance is familiar: I often distance myself. The difference I noticed in the rapid to and fro of talk was that, whereas I used to move at will in and out of this no-man's-land by simply changing my focus in a quick, smooth run of attention, last night, among young people of high ambition, mottles of rust seemed to catch on the wheels of this familiar mechanism. I actually found myself hoping that they were not squeaking audibly. I had to make a real effort to adjust to the rapid give and take, and once or twice envisioned the possibility of a retirement—not of choice but of failure. Perhaps a chill, bony touch of age on my shoulder.

The other day I caught my mirror image in a casual side glance and saw to my surprise a person older than I feel. Thin, delicate-tissued, with a drift of fine gray hair.

AUGUST

Mary brought me back some postcards from the Louvre when she returned from her trip to Paris last fall. Whistler's *Portrait of the Artist's Mother* was among them, and I hold it in my hand now and marvel at the perfection of Whistler's art, betrayed in this painting only by a fatal empathy for the values that apparently led his mother to a resignation so somber as to have habitually affected her son's palette. From every point of view except the psychological, a flawless "arrangement in black and white," a delicious counterpoint of delicacy and austerity. But the flaccid acceptance of his mother's character, the incapacity or unwillingness to look beyond her persona—which allows Whistler to use her in his composition as he would any other object, tenderly as he does so—fatally reduces the impact of the painting. Rembrandt would never have let his mother get away so easily. Confronting her eye to eye, he would have caught the glint of her individual authenticity, and in that glint refracted from the pigment on his brush the indomitable humanity that remains forever aloof from convention.

The summer of my sixtieth year is dappled with sun and shadow. Even as I rejoiced to watch with Alexandra while Sammy and my new puppy cavorted in the garden trying to catch fireflies, memories of other evanescent summer nights reminded me of mortality. In a way that is reminiscent of my early twenties, I am caught by the refraction from some deep, dark, and tender mirror that deflects the personal toward the universal. From this fixed point, experiences look like examples of experience. Yet, the springs of my affections are so fresh that I have little taste for the perspective this distance gives me. I wish that those I love dearly should have more than I have had myself.

SEPTEMBER

Summer has run out. I am alone again. The visits of my children and grandchildren have been, in the disarming form of sheer delight, bittersweet, evoking a poignant review of my life. As I lived it, I felt it so entirely unique—not that I thought myself unique but that the moments as I advanced in them each struck a note I had not before experienced—that to see the pattern repeated in detail after detail is humbling. My children's lives seem gently but inexorably to round my own as if enclosing it in a crystal ball wherein I see it entire. And see clearly what I have until now seen only darkly: that what is done is past, spun out of me in a few threads, scarcely discernible, woven into the immense generalization of human life.

I believe that I return so persistently to the insights of my childhood because what I think of as my nerve in art had its origin at that time in my first recognition that I was alien in the universe. And I believe that because this realization of alienness ground itself into my mind in that particular setting, its characteristics became highly charged for me. I turned to this setting, away from the void. It was a choice of life over death. So that certain band of experience—the landscape of my childhood in all its inflections—became entirely providentially the nearest to home I am ever likely to know on this earth. Within these inflections lies the range of my sensitivity.

YADDO. I write in Yaddo's Stone South studio once more, glancing out now and then over the autumn berry bushes into the familiar meadow and apple trees, now so richly laden that their dark trunks rise from circles of fallen fruit, the pale, clear green of sun in a curling wave.

When I stayed at Aunt Nancy's farm in Virginia as a young girl, it was my job to separate the milk every morning and evening. I used to marvel that all I had to do was to assemble, carefully and with very clean hands, a well-scrubbed device and turn the crank for cream to emerge. I never understood how the mechanism worked; nor do I understand why the simple act of writing has so apparently effortlessly revealed to me the secret logic of my life. And, in that logic, a faith to illuminate my days.

Acknowledgments

This book would not have come to publication without the sensitive and steadfast encouragement of Margot Backas, whose faith in the manuscript has over and over again sustained me in my effort. I am grateful to Julia Randall for introducing me to her. I am also grateful to Jean V. Naggar, my literary agent, for her resolute loyalty. I thank Dale Loy for introducing me to Nan Graham, who has been an extraordinarily generous editor; her sensibility and intelligence have been illuminating.

Much of this writing was done at Yaddo. I am immeasurably grateful for my visits there, for reasons both practical and ineffable. And I thank the Ossabaw Foundation for my stay on the island.

My children, Alexandra, Mary, and Sam are the greatest blessings of my life. This book is theirs, by right of the lovely affection with which they surrounded me while I was writing it.

About the Author

Anne Truitt was born in Baltimore in 1921 and grew up on Maryland's Eastern Shore. She received a BA in psychology from Bryn Mawr College in 1943. In 1947 she married James Truitt and moved to Washington, D.C., where, in 1949, she commenced the study of art at the Institute for Contemporary Art. Her English translation of Germaine Bree's *Du Temps Perdu au Temps Retrouvé: Marcel Proust and Deliverance from Time* was published by Rutgers University Press in 1955.

The André Emmerich Gallery in New York held the first solo exhibition of Anne Truitt's sculptures in 1963. Since then her sculptures, paintings, and drawings have been the subject of museum and gallery exhibitions in Tokyo, London, and throughout the United States, including major surveys at the Corcoran Gallery of Art and the Hirshhorn Museum and Sculpture Garden in Washington, D.C., and the Whitney Museum of American Art in New York.

Anne Truitt taught art at the University of Maryland from 1975 to 1996, and she traveled extensively as a visiting artist and lecturer. Her distinctions include fellowships from Yaddo, the John Simon Guggenheim Memorial Foundation, the National Endowment for the Arts, and the Australia Arts Council. She received honorary doctorates from the Kansas City Art Institute, Kansas; St. Mary's College of Maryland; the Maryland Institute College of Art, Baltimore; and Parsons New School for Social Research, New York. In 2003 the University of Nebraska awarded her the Cather Medal for service to humanity.

During the 1950s Anne Truitt had three children. In 1964 the family moved to Japan, where James Truitt worked as *Newsweek* magazine's Far East bureau chief. Three years later they returned to Washington, D.C., which remained Anne Truitt's home until her death in 2004.

Anne Truitt's work is in the collections of the Metropolitan Museum of Art, the Museum of Modern Art, and the Whitney Museum of American Art in New York; the National Gallery of Art, the Hirshhorn Museum and Sculpture Garden, and the Smithsonian American Art Museum in Washington, D.C.; the Albright-Knox Art Gallery in Buffalo, New York; the Walker Art Center in Minneapolis; and numerous other museums. The Estate of Anne Truitt is represented by Matthew Marks Gallery, New York.